HISTORY OF KANNADA LITERATURE

HISTORY OF KANNADA LITERATURE

(READERSHIP LECTURES)

R. NARASIMHACHARYA

GYAN

Published by

Gyan Publishing House
5, Ansari Road
Daryaganj, New Delhi-110002
Phone: 011-47034999, 9811692060
E-mail: books@gyanbooks.com

Distribution Network
gyanbooks.com
India, USA, Canada, UK, Australia, France

ISBN : 978-81-212-3523-5 (PB)

2nd Impression 2020

Printed at: Gyan Press, Delhi.

History of Kannada Literature
Author: R. Narasimhacharya

CONTENTS

CHAPTER I

Antiquity of Kannaḍa Literature

CHAPTER II

Poets and Poetry

CHAPTER III

Connection of Kannaḍa Literature with those of Telugu, Tamil and Sanskrit

CHAPTER III (*Contd.*)

CHAPTER IV

SOME CRITICISMS ANSWERED

CHAPTER V

EXTENT AND RANGE OF KANNAḌA LITERATURE

CHAPTER I

ANTIQUITY OF KANNAḌA LITERATURE

As compared with that of the Sister Languages of Southern India

SOME scholars have suggested that there may have been a Buddhist period in Kannaḍa literature before the Jaina period. The same suggestion has also been made by some Telugu scholars with regard to their literature and it has been said that Buddhist works have been completely lost in Telugu, though a very few Jaina works have survived. The Tamils do not divide their literature into Buddhist, Jaina and other periods, because their literature contains works by Buddhist and Jaina authors at different times. With regard to Buddhist works in Tamil, it may be said that they are very few; and they occur along with works of Jainas and others at different periods till the 11th century. As instances there may be mentioned *Maṇimēkhalai* and *Kuṇḍalakēśi*, two of the five great *kāvyas* in Tamil, which go back to the Sangam period, and the grammar *Vīraśōḷiyam* of the 11th century.

Whether there was a Buddhist period in Kannaḍa or no, its literature, such as it is, is of considerable antiquity, though no sages like Agastya and Kaṇva, as in Tamil and Telugu respectively, are associated with its origin. The earliest work extant is a treatise on poetics called *Kavirājamārga* by Nṛipatuṅga or Amōghavarsha, the Rāsṭrakūṭa king who ruled from 815 to 877. This king was a great scholar both in Kannaḍa and Sanskrit and a great patron of literary merit. He has written in Sanskrit a small work called *Praśnōttararatnamālā*, of which the concluding verse tells us that he voluntarily retired from the throne.[1] It may be of some interest to learn that

[1] ವಿವೇಕಾತ್ತ್ಯಕ್ತ ರಾಜ್ಯೇನ ರಾಜ್ಞೇಯಂ ರತ್ನಮಾಲಿಕಾ |
ರಚಿತಾಮೋಘವರ್ಷೇಣ ಸುಧಿಯಾ ಸದಲಂಕೃತಿಃ ||

Ugrāditya, the Jaina author of *Kalyāṇakāraka*, a Sanskrit work on medicine, says at the close of the work that at the instance of this king he delivered at his court, in the presence of many physicians and doctors, a discourse on the evils of a flesh diet and on its avoidance in the treatment of disease. Nṛipatuṅga was a Jaina king, a disciple of Jinasēna, the author of *Ādipurāṇa*. His work on poetics presupposes the existence of previous Kannaḍa works, and accordingly we find references in it which enable us to place the rise of Kannaḍa literature much farther back. He mentions several Kannaḍa authors that preceded him: Vimala, Udaya, Nāgārjuna, Jayabandhu and Durvinīta as the best writers of Kannaḍa prose; and Srīvijaya, Kavīśvara, Paṇḍita, Chandra and Lōkapāla as the best writers of Kannaḍa poetry. Durvinīta, mentioned as a Kannaḍa prose writer, was evidently the Ganga king of that name. The name Durvinīta, being rare and unusual, may safely be taken to refer to the Ganga king, the only inscription in which the name occurs outside Ganga grants being Māgaḍi 75, of 966, about a century after Nṛipatuṅga's time. Durvinīta was a remarkable personage with many-sided scholarship.[1]

The *Avantisundarīkathāsāra*, discovered some years ago by the Madras Oriental Manuscripts Library, gives a valuable clue to the period of Durvinīta. In the introductory chapter it says that Bhāravi stayed for some time at the court of Durvinīta and that he was a contemporary of Vishṇuvardhana, evidently the first Eastern Chālukya king, and of Simhavishṇu, the Pallava king of Kānchi. Briefly, the account given of Bhāravi runs thus:--In the

[1] His Nallāla plates (*Mysore Archæological Report* for 1924, p. 70), describe his scholarship thus:

ಅನೇಕ ಕಾವ್ಯ, ಕಥಾ ನಾಟಕ ಪ್ರಣಯನ ಪ್ರರೂಢ ಪಾಟವೇನ, ನೀತಿಶಾಸ್ತ್ರ ಗ್ರಂಥಾರ್ಥ ಪ್ರಯೋಗ ಪ್ರತಿಪಾದನಂ ಪ್ರತಿ ಪ್ರತ್ಯಕ್ಷ ವಿಷ್ಣುಗುಪ್ತೇನ, ಗಾಂಧರ್ವ ನಾಟ್ಯ ಶಾಸ್ತ್ರ ವ್ಯಾಖ್ಯಾನ ವಿನಿಯೋಗಂ ಪ್ರತಿ ಸಮತಿಶಯಿತ ತುಂಬರು ನಾರದ ಭರತ ಕಂಬಳಾಚಾರ್ಯೇಣ, ಹಸ್ತಿಶಿಕ್ಷಾಶ್ವ ಶಿಕ್ಷಾ ವಿಜ್ಞಾನ ವಿನಿಯೋಜನಂ ಪ್ರತಿ ಸಮತುಲಿತ ರಾಜಪುತ್ರ ಶಾಲಿಹೋತ್ರೇಣ, ಅಸ್ತ್ರೋಪಾಸ್ತ್ರ ವಿಪ್ರಹರಣ ವಿದ್ಯಾಭಿಯೋಗಂ ಪ್ರತಿ ಸಮಕ್ಷೀಕೃತ ಪರಶುರಾಮೇಣ, ಪುರುಷ ಲಕ್ಷಣ ಶಾಸ್ತ್ರ ವಿಧೌ ಪ್ರತಿ ಸಾಕ್ಷಾತ್ಸಮುದ್ರಸೂರಿಣಾ, ಆಯುರ್ವೇದ ವಿಜ್ಞಾನಂ ಪ್ರತಿ ಸದ್ಯಶಾತ್ರೇಯ ಧನ್ವಂತರೀ ಚರಕೇನ, ಅರಿ ನರಪತಿ ಶ್ರೀ ದುರ್ವಿನೀತ ನಾಮಧೇಯೇನ.

city of Kānchi in the south of India ruled a king of the Pallavas named Simhavishṇu who was a great patron of learning. One day a stranger appeared before him and recited a Sanskrit verse in praise of the Narasimha incarnation of Vishṇu. On hearing the lofty sentiments expressed in the verse the king enquired of the stranger who the author of the verse was. He replied thus: 'In the north-west there is a town named Ānandapura, the crest-jewel of Āryadēśa, from which a family of Brāhmaṇas of the Kauśika-gōtra migrated and settled at Achalapura. Nārāyaṇasvāmi, a member of this family, had a son named Dāmōdara, who became a great scholar and was known as Bhāravi. He became a friend of king Vishṇuvardhana. On one occasion he accompanied the king on a hunting expedition and while in the forest had to eat animal flesh. To expiate this sin he set out on a pilgrimage and finally settled in the court of Durvinīta. He is the author of this verse.' On hearing this account the king, desirous of seeing the poet, invited him to his court. The poet caused great joy to the king by reciting his poems. The king gave him a respectable dwelling to live in and supplied all his wants.

This extract establishes the contemporaneity of the Pallava king Simhavishṇu (c. 575–600), the Ganga king Durvinīta and the Eastern Chālukya king Vishṇuvardhana (I). This association of Durvinīta with Bhāravi affords a clear explanation of the statement in most of the Ganga grants that Durvinīta was the author of a commentary on the fifteenth Sarga of Bhāravi's *Kirātārjunīya*. When Bhāravi was with him, Durvinīta might have exercised his skill in commenting on the fifteenth Sarga of his work, which is full of alliteration and other forms of *sabdālankāra* or verbal ornaments and is consequently difficult of comprehension without a commentary. The period of Durvinīta according to the newly discovered work will thus be about 600.

As stated before, Durvinīta was a great Sanskrit scholar. He wrote, according to the Ganga grants, a grammatical work named *Śabdāvatāra*, a commentary on Pānini's Grammar, and translated into Sanskrit the

Paiśāchi Vaḍḍakathā or *Bṛihatkathā* of Guṇāḍhya as the epithet applied to him in the Ganga grants, viz., *Dēva-bhāratī-nibaddha-Bṛihatkathaḥ*, clearly shows. This epithet was not properly read and understood by some scholars who read it *Dēvabhāratī-nibaddha-Bṛihatpathaḥ* and interpreted it as meaning that Durvinīta was a disciple of Dēva or Dēvanandi, a name of Pūjyapāda. It is to be regretted that his translation has not come down to us. It happens to be the earliest Sanskrit translation of Guṇāḍhya's work. There are three later translations of this work, namely, *Bṛihatkathāślōkasaṅgraha* by Budhasvāmi, of about the 8th century; *Bṛihatkathā-mañjari* by Kshēmēndra, and *Kathāsaritsāgara* by Sōmadēva, both of the 11th century. Budhasvāmi's work has been published in Paris by Professor Felix Lacote, Professor of Sanskrit in the University of Lyon. The period we have already arrived at for Durvinīta is corroborated by an inscription at Aihoḷe (*Epigraphia Indica*, VI, 1-12). This epigraph was composed in 634 A.D. by a Jaina poet named Ravikīrti, who speaks of himself as having acquired the fame of Kālidāsa and Bhāravi in poetical skill.[1] (Kavitāśrita-Kālidāsa-Bhāravi-Kīrtih.) For the fame of Bhāravi as a great poet to spread to the south we have to postulate a period of about half a century, and this fact, too, confirms the period of Durvinīta as about 600.

Kannaḍa inscriptions make their appearance from about the 5th century, which indicate an older stage of the language, as will be shown later on, than that found in *Kavirājamārga*. Besides the authors named by Nṛipatuṅga, Śyāmakundāchārya appears, according to Indranandi's *Śrutāvatāra*,[2] to have written *Prābhṛita* in Kannaḍa.

When speaking of the greatness of the Kannaḍa language in his *Śabdānuśāsana*, Bhaṭṭākalanka (1604) says: 'Nor is Karṇāṭaka a language unused for scientific

[1] ಕವಿತಾಶ್ರಿತ ಕಾಲಿದಾಸ ಭಾರವಿಕೀರ್ತಿಃ.

[2] ಕಾಲೇ ತತಃ ಕಿಯತ್ಯಪಿಗತೇ ಪುನಃ ಶ್ಯಾಮಕುಂದಸಂಜ್ಞೇನ |
ಪ್ರಾಕೃತ ಸಂಸ್ಕೃತ ಕರ್ಣಾಟಭಾಷಯಾ ಪದ್ಧತಿಃ ಪರಾ ರಚಿತಾ ||

purposes. For, in it was written the great work called *Chūḍāmaṇi*, 96,000 verse-measures in extent, a commentary on the *Tattvārthamahāśāstra*.'[1] And from Indranandi's *Śrutāvatāra*[2] and Dēvachandra's *Rājāvalīkathe*, we learn that the author of this voluminous Kannaḍa commentary was Tumbulūrāchārya, who, judging from the pedigree of Jaina gurus given at the end of *Chāmuṇḍarāyapurāṇa* (978), appears to have lived along with the above-mentioned Śyāmakundāchārya in about the middle of the 7th century. This voluminous work of the 7th century presupposes the existence of an earlier literature and a widespread cultivation of the language.

From the Śravaṇa Beḷgoḷa inscription 67, of 1129, we learn that Śrīvardhadēva, a crest-jewel of poets, was the author of a great poem named *Chūḷāmaṇi* and that he was thus praised by Daṇḍi.[3] Śiva bore the Ganga on the tip of his matted hair. O Śrīvardhadēva! you bear Sarasvati on the tip of your tongue! From the similarity of the name Chūḍāmaṇi, Śrīvardhadēva has been identified with Tumbulūrāchārya. But this, I am inclined to think, is a mistake. The great poem *Chūḷāmaṇi* and the commentary *Chūḍāmaṇi* cannot be the same. I venture to think that the reference is to the Tamil poem *Chūḷāmaṇi* attributed to Tōlāmoḷidēvar, otherwise known as Śrīvardhadēvar. *Chūḷāmaṇi* is a classical Jaina poem in Tamil, considered as one of the five well-known minor poems in that language, written during the rule of the Kārveṭṭi king Vijaya, whose period is not definitely known.

[1] ನಚೈಷಾ (ಕರ್ಣಾಟಭಾಷಾ) ಶಾಸ್ತ್ರಾನುಪಯೋಗಿನೀ ; ತತ್ತ್ವಾರ್ಥ ಮಹಾಶಾಸ್ತ್ರ ವ್ಯಾಖ್ಯಾನಸ್ಯ ಷಣ್ಣವತಿಸಹಸ್ರಪ್ರಮಿತ ಗ್ರಂಥಸಂದರ್ಭರೂಪಸ್ಯ ಚೂಡಾಮಣ್ಯಭಿಧಾನಸ್ಯ ಮಹಾಶಾಸ್ತ್ರಸ್ಯ . . . ಉಪಲಭ್ಯಮಾನತ್ವಾತ್.

[2] ಕರ್ಣಾಟಭಾಷಯಾ ಕೃತ ಮಹತೀಂ ಚೂಡಾಮಣಿಂ ವ್ಯಾಖ್ಯಾಂ.

[3] ಚೂಳಾಮಣಿಃ ಕವೀನಾಂ ಚೂಳಾಮಣಿನಾಮಸೇವ್ಯಕಾವ್ಯಕವಿಃ |
ಶ್ರೀವರ್ಧದೇವ ಏವಹಿ ಕೃತಪುಣ್ಯಃ ಕೀರ್ತಿಮಾಹರ್ತುಂ ||

ಯ ಏವಮುಪಶ್ಲೋಕಿತೋ ದಂಡಿನಾ :—
ಜಹ್ನೋಃ ಕನ್ಯಾಂ ಜಟಾಗ್ರೇಣ ಬಭಾರ ಪರಮೇಶ್ವರಃ |
ಶ್ರೀವರ್ಧದೇವ ಸಂಧತ್ಸೇ ಜಿಹ್ವಾಗ್ರೇಣ ಸರಸ್ವತೀಂ ||

It has been stated above that Kannaḍa inscriptions of an earlier period than Kavirājamārga show an older stage of the language. To illustrate this statement I give below some extracts from early inscriptions:

Early Inscriptions prior to Nṛipatuṅga's Period

1. CHIKMAGAḶŪR 50 (c. 500).
   ನಿರ್ವ್ವಿನೀತರಾ ಕಿಱಿಯಾ ಮಗನ್ದಿರ್ ಪಟ್ಟಸೂಡಿದೋರ್.

2. SRAVAṆA BEḶGOḶA 27 (c. 700).
   ಮಾಸೇನರ್ ಪರಮಪ್ರಭಾವರುಷಿಯರ್ ಕಟ್ವಪ್ಪಿನಾ ವೆಟ್ಟದುಳ್
   ಶ್ರೀ ಸಂಘಂಗಳ ಪೇೞ್ದ ಸಿದ್ಧ ಸಮಯಂ ತಪಸ್ಸಾದೆ ನೋಂತಿಂಬಿನಿನ್ |
   ಪ್ರಾಸಾದಾಂತರಮಾನ್ ವಿಚಿತ್ರ ಕನಕಪ್ರಜ್ವಲ್ಯದಿನ್ ಮಿಕ್ಕುದಾನ್
   ಸಾಸಿರ್ವರ್ ವರಪೂಜೆದಂದುಯೆ ಅವರ್ ಸ್ವರ್ಗಾಗ್ರಮಾಸೇಱಿದಾರ್ ||

3. CHIKMAGAḶŪR 92 (c. 750).
   ಇದಾನ್ ನಾಡಾಳ್ವೋನಾನುಂ ಊರಾಳ್ವೋನಾನುಂ ಊರಾ ಒಕ್ಕಲಾನುಂ ಅೞಿವೋರ್ ಪಞ್ಚಮಹಾಪಾತಕಯುಕ್ತರ್.

4. KAḌŪR 45 (c. 750).
   ಒರ್ವರ್ಳ್ಳನೆಯ್ಮ್ಮಱಿಸಿದಾನ್ ಕಿಡಿಸಿದೋನುಂ ಬಾರಣಾಸಿಯುಳ್ ಪಾತಕಂ ಗೆಯ್ದೋನ ಸಂದ ಗತಿಗೆ ಸಲ್ವೋನ್.

In these extracts we find many archaic forms not found in *Kavirājamārga* and works that followed it. In fact the language of Nṛipatuṅga scarcely differs from that of the later authors of the 10th and 11th centuries. The inscriptions show:

1. A general use of the lengthened form of the vowel of the genitive:
   ನಿರ್ವ್ವಿನೀತರಾ, ಕಟ್ವಪ್ಪಿನಾ, ಊರಾ.

2. The use of the locative suffix *uḷ* for the later *oḷ*:
   ವೆಟ್ಟದುಳ್, ಬಾರಣಾಸಿಯುಳ್.

3. A general use of the lengthened form of the vowel of the accusative, even when followed by a consonant:
   ಪ್ರಾಸಾದಾಂತರಮಾನ್, ಮಿಕ್ಕುದಾನ್, ಸ್ವರ್ಗಾಗ್ರಮಾನ್, ಇದಾನ್.

4. The use of *n* for the later *bindu*: ಇಂಬಿನಿನ್, ಪ್ರಜ್ವಲ್ಯದಿನ್; see also examples under (3).

5. The use of the long vowel instead of the later short vowel in ತಪ್ಪಾದೆ and ಕಿಱಯಾ.

6. The general use of the lengthened form of the vowel of the conjugational suffixes:

ಏಱದಾರ್, ಅಟಿದೋರ್, ನಿಱಸಿದಾಳ್, ಕಿಡಿಸಿದೋಳ್, ಅಕ್ಕೋಳ್ ಗೆಯ್ದೋಳ್, ಸಲ್ತೋಳ್.

Tamil Literature

No one entertains a doubt about the antiquity of Tamil literature, but this antiquity depends to a great extent on the period assigned to the authors and works of the third Saṅgam.

According to tradition there were three Tamil Saṅgams or Academies at long intervals in different places. The following particulars are given about them in Nakkīrar's commentary on Iṟaiyanār's *Agapporul*:—

The first academy was established at Southern Madura, now submerged in the Indian ocean. Its members were 549 in number, including among others Agastya, its president, and the gods Śiva and Subrahmaṇya; and the number of authors who obtained its approval for their works was 4,449. It was patronised by 89 Pāṇḍya kings, of whom 7 were also poets, and lasted for 4,440 years.

The second academy had its seat at Kapāṭapuram, also submerged in the ocean. Its members, including Agastya, his disciple Tolkāppiya and others, were 59 in number, the number of poets whose works were passed by it being 3,700. It received the patronage of 59 Pāṇḍya kings, 5 of whom were also learned scholars, and continued for 3,700 years.

The third academy was founded at Northern Madura. Its members were 49 in number, including Nakkīrar, its president, Kapilar, Paraṇar, Śīttalai Śāttanār and others, the number of authors who obtained its approval for their writings being 449. It was patronised by 49 Pāṇḍya kings, 3 of whom were also poets, and lasted for 1,850 years.

If the facts stated above be subjected to strict historical criticism, most of them will have to be rejected as pure myths. The number of members of the academies and of the kings who patronised them, as also of the poets whose works were passed by them, and the long periods during which they are said to have existed, look incredible. Some scholars are therefore inclined to think that the account given above is a later fabrication foisted on the early author Nakkīrar. Kavāṭapuram of the Pāṇḍyas is, however, mentioned in *Vālmīki-Rāmāyaṇa* as full of gold and adorned with pearls[1] and must therefore be an ancient city. The existence of the academies may be a fact, though the details given about them may not be credible. They exercised a great authority over Tamil literature and were something like literary associations including among its members the best poets and learned men of the age. Any work not approved of by them was looked upon as a very inferior production. The members of these learned corporations maintained a strict monopoly of literary reputation so that it was not an easy matter to have works, however excellent, recognised by them. According to some scholars the accounts of the first two academies contain much legendary matter so that it is difficult to admit them within the pale of real history. Such, however, does not seem to them to be the case with the third academy. The third academy was by far the most important, almost all the classical works of Tamil literature that have come down to us, including a good number by Jaina authors, being productions which received the *imprimatur* of this Saṅgam.

Opinion is divided among scholars about the period of the third Saṅgam, some assigning to it the second century A.D., some the 5th century and others the 8th century. The 2nd century is arrived at by the fact that Gajabāhu, a king of Ceylon who ruled in the middle of the 2nd century, was, according to the poem *Silappadikāram* present at the installation of the Goddess

[1] ತತೋ ಹೇಮಮಯಂ ದಿವ್ಯಂ ಮುಕ್ತಾಮಣಿವಿಭೂಷಿತಂ |
ಯುಕ್ತಂ ಕವಾಟಂ ಪಾಂಡ್ಯಾನಾಂ ಗತಾ ದ್ರಕ್ಷ್ಯಥ ವಾನರಾಃ ||
ಕಿಷ್ಕಿಂಧಾಕಾಂಡ, 41, 19.

Pattini conducted by the Chēra king Śenguṭṭuvan. The 8th century is objected to on the ground that Nakkīrar. a poet of the third Saṅgam, is referred to in his *Dēvāram* by Appar, a contemporary of Siruttoṇḍar who fought at the battle of Vātāpi which took place in 642. The balance of opinion among Tamil scholars appears to be in favour of the Gajabāhu synchronism, which will carry back the antiquity of Tamil literature to the earliest centuries of the Christian era.

But Śīttalai Sāttanār, author of the Tamil epic *Maṇimēkhalai*, which is considered to be a work of the third Saṅgam, and has been assigned by several Tamil scholars to the 2nd century, has regularly translated Diṅnāga's *Nyāyapravēsa* in lines 110 to 474 of the chapter known as *Tavattiṛampūṇḍu tarumam Kēṭṭa Kādai* of his work. So he must be posterior to Diṅnāga who is supposed to be not earlier than the 4th century. But Tamil scholars may say that both the authors may have derived the information from an earlier common source. This is not, however, likely, as the following extracts from the Tamil and Sanskrit works will show the only difference being a few additional explanatory words in the Tamil passage:

I. ll. 122-24.

ಏತು ಮೂನ್ಱಾಯ್ತ್ತೋನ್ಱುಮವೈಟಾನ್ ಪಕ್ಕ ತ್ತುನ್ಱು ನಿಱ್ಱಲುಂ ಸಪಕ್ಕತ್ತುಣ್ಡಾದಲುಂ ವಿಪಕ್ಕತ್ತಿನ್ಱಿಯೇ ವಿಡುತಲುಂ	ಹೇತುಸ್ತ್ರಿರೂಪಃ | ಕಿಂ ಪುನಸ್ತ್ರೈರೂಪ್ಯಂ | ಪಕ್ಷಧರ್ಮತ್ವಂ ಸಪಕ್ಷೇ ಸತ್ವಂ ವಿಪಕ್ಷೇ ಚಾಸತ್ವಮಿತಿ |

II. ll. 147-171.

ಪಕ್ಕಪ್ಪೋಲಿಯೊನ್ಱದು ವಕೈಪ್ಪಡುಮ್ ಪಿರತ್ತಿಯಕ್ಕ ವಿರುತ್ತಮನುಮಾನ ವಿರುತ್ತಂಸುವಚನವಿರುತ್ತಮುಲೋಕ ವಿರುತ್ತಮಾಗಮವಿರುತ್ತಮಪ್ಪಿರ ಶಿತ್ತವಿಶೇಡಣಮಪ್ಪಿರಶಿತ್ತ ವಿಶೇಡಿಯಮಪ್ಪಿರಶಿತ್ತವುಬಯ	ಪಕ್ಷಾಭಾಸಾಃ ನವ | ತದ್ಯಥಾ— ಪ್ರತ್ಯಕ್ಷವಿರುದ್ಧಃ, ಅನುಮಾನವಿರುದ್ಧಃ, ಆಗಮವಿರುದ್ಧಃ, ಸ್ವವಚನವಿರುದ್ಧಃ, ಲೋಕವಿರುದ್ಧಃ, ಅಪ್ರಸಿದ್ಧವಿಶೇಷಣಃ, ಅಪ್ರಸಿದ್ಧವಿಶೇಷ್ಯಃ, ಅಪ್ರಸಿದ್ಧೋ ಭಯಃ,

ಮಪ್ಪಿರಶಿತ್ತಶಮ್ಬನ್ದಮ್ಮೆನ
ವೆಣ್ಣೆಯುವಿವಱ್ಱಿರತ್ತಿಯಕ್ಕವಿರುತ್ತ
ಜ್ಗಣ್ಣೆಯು ಕಾಟ್ಚಿ ಮಾಱುಕೊಳಲಾಗು
ಇಜ್ಜತ್ತಿಜ್ಜಿ ವಿಕಸ್ಪುಪ್ಪುಲನನ್ಱೆನ
ಮಱ್ಱಿನುಮಾನವಿರುತ್ತಮಾವದು
ಕರುತ್ತಳವೈಯ್ಯೆ ಮಾಱಾಗಕ್ಕೊಱ
ಲನಿತ್ತಿಯಕ್ಕಡತ್ತೈ ನಿತ್ತಿಯಮೆನ್ಱಲ್
ಶುವಶನವಿರುತ್ತನ್ದ ಶೊನ್ಮಾಱುಪಡು
ಯಮ್ಬ
ಲೆನ್ಱಾಯ್ ಮಲಡಿಯೆನ್ಱೇಮಿಯಮ್ಬಲ್
ಆಗಮವಿರುತ್ತನ್ಗನ್ಮಾನಾತ್ತಱೈದ
ಲನಿತ್ತವಾದಿಯಾಯುಳ್ಳ ವೈಶೇಡಿಕ
ನನಿತ್ತಿಯತ್ತೈ ನಿತ್ತಿಯಮೆನ ನುವಱ
ಲಪ್ಪಿರಶಿತ್ತ ವಿಶೇಡಣಮಾವದು
ತತ್ತಮೆದಿರುಕ್ಕಿಚ್ಚಾತ್ತಿಯನ್ಗಿರಿ
ಯಾವ್ವೈ
ಪೌತ್ತನ್ಮಾಡಾಯ್ನಿನ್ಱ ಶಾಙ್ಕಿಯನ್ಱೆ
ಕ್ಕಱಿತ್ತುಜ್ಜತ್ತುಮ್ ವಿನಾಶಿಯೆನ್ಱಲ್

ಪ್ರಸಿದ್ಧ[1]ಸಂಬಂಧಶ್ಚೇತಿ |
ತತ್ರ ಪ್ರತ್ಯಕ್ಷವಿರುದ್ಧೋ ಯಥಾ—
ಅಶ್ರಾವಣಃ ಶಬ್ದ ಇತಿ |
ಅನುಮಾನವಿರುದ್ಧೋ ಯಥಾ—
ನಿತ್ಯೋ ಘಟ ಇತಿ |
ಸ್ವವಚನವಿರುದ್ಧೋ ಯಥಾ—
ಮಾತಾ ಮೇ ವಂಧ್ಯಾ |
ಆಗಮವಿರುದ್ಧೋ ಯಥಾ—ವೈಶೇಷಿಕಸ್ಯ
ನಿತ್ಯಶ್ಶಬ್ದ ಇತಿ ಸಾಧಯತಃ |
ಅಪ್ರಸಿದ್ಧ ವಿಶೇಷಣೋ ಯಥಾ-ಬೌದ್ಧಸ್ಯ
ಸಾಂಖ್ಯಂ ಪ್ರತಿ ವಿನಾಶೀ ಶಬ್ದ ಇತಿ |[2]

If the period assigned to Diṅnāga is correct, the period of *Maṇimēkhali* and consequently the period of the third Saṅgam will probably be the 5th century.

Telugu Literature

The earliest work extant in Telugu is the *Bhārata* of Nannayya-bhaṭṭa, the court poet of the Eastern Chālukya king Rājarāja (1023–63). He is generally considered to be the first poet in that language.[3] But, as in the case of Kannaḍa, poetical inscriptions of an earlier period have been found such as those of the Eastern Chālukya king Guṇaga-Vijayāditya (844–88) in Ongole

[1] I am told that some Tibetan manuscripts have the reading ಅಪ್ರಸಿದ್ಧ.

[2] I am indebted to Mr. H. R. Rangaswamiengar, M.A., of the Oriental Library, for the Sanskrit extracts.

[3] ವಾಚಾಮಾಂಧ್ರಮಯೀನಾಂ ಯಃ ಪ್ರವಕ್ತಾ ಪ್ರಥಮೋಭವತ್ |
ಆಚಾರ್ಯಂ ತಂ ಕವೀಂದ್ರಾಣಾಂ ವಂದೇ ವಾಗನುಶಾಸನಂ ||

Taluk (Madras *Epigraphical Report* for 1923) and the pillar inscription at Bezwāḍa of the Eastern Chālukya King Yuddhamalla who ruled in the early part of the 10th century. Nannayya-bhaṭṭa also happens to be the first grammarian of the Telugu language, and grammar presupposes the existence of previous literature.

Malayāḷam Literature

With regard to Malayāḷam literature, the scholars of that language say that up to the 10th century the language of Kēraḷa was Śendamiḻ, i.e., pure Tamil. Omitting *maṇipravāḷam* works, *Rāmacharitam* by Śrī-Rāma, a Travancore king of the 13th century, is the earliest work in Malayāḷam literature. In Malayāḷam *maṇipravāḷam* works not only Sanskrit words but also Sanskrit case endings were freely combined with Malayāḷam words.[1] The real secret of *maṇipravāḷam* according to Malayāḷam scholars lay in the blending of Malayāḷam and Sanskrit words in such a manner as to make the latter indistinguishable from the former, exactly as the intermingling of the ruby and the coral in one and the same necklace. Tuñjattu Eḻuttachchan of the 16th century is considered as the father of modern Malayāḷam (classical) literature. I may add that there are *maṇipravāḷa* works in Tamil also.

It will thus be seen that the literature of Kannaḍa is of far greater antiquity than that of any other South Indian, or for that matter, any other Indian, vernacular, except perhaps that of Tamil.

[1] As instances I give two verses from *Śrīkṛishṇacharitam:*
അത്രാന്തരേ തത്ര സമീപവാസീ സത്രാജിതാഖ്യൻ കില യാദവേന്ദ്രൻ |
മിത്രപ്രസാദേന മുദാ ലഭിച്ചാൻ മിത്രപ്രകാശോപമമേകരത്നം ||
വൈകുണ്ഠദേവ നിജഗോക്കളെ മേച്ചു ദിനാന്ത്യേ പോകുന്ന ദിന്ന ബഹു സങ്കടമംഗനാനാം |
കൃഷ്ണൻ വരുന്ന വടിസോക്തി വസിക്ക്യമേഷ്ഠം തൃഷ്ണാവശേന വിവശാ ദിവസാവസാനേ ||
I am obliged to Mr. P. R. Subrahmanya Sastri, B.A., for these extracts.

CHAPTER II

POETS AND POETRY

NṚIPATUṄGA (815-77) in his *Kavirājamārga* gives the uses of Kāvya in the following verse (I, 18):

ಪಾಪಮಿದು ಪುಣ್ಯಮಿದು ಹಿತ| ರೂಪಮಿದಹಿತಪ್ರಕಾರಮಿದು ಸುಖಮಿದು ದುಃ|
ಖೋಪಾತ್ತಮಿದೆಂದಱಿವುಗು | ಮಾ ಪರಮಕವಿಪ್ರಧಾನರಾ ಕಾವ್ಯಂಗಳ್ ||

He mentions two kinds of composition (I, 32, 34 and 35), *bedaṇḍe* and *chattāna*, with the remark that they were recognised by early poets. The former is defined as a composition consisting of alternate *kandas* and *vrittas*, and the latter as one consisting of many *kandas* along with *vrittas*, *akkara*, *chaupadi*, *gītika* and *tivadi*. He states (I, 50) that Hala-Gannaḍa is quite appropriate in ancient poems, but insipid in works of the present time like association with an old woman. According to him mixture of Kannaḍa with Sanskrit is harsh to the ear (1, 52), but mixture of Kannaḍa with Sama-Samskṛita is pleasant to the ear like music (I, 54), while mixture of Kannaḍa and Sanskrit in compounds is disagreeable like mixing drops of buttermilk with boiling milk (I, 57). He condemns unnecessary use of expletives such as *ante*, *matte*, *gadam*, etc., in the following verse (II, 12):

ಇನ್ನಂತೆ ಮತ್ತೆ ಬಟಿ ಮಿಗೆ| ಮುಂ ನಿಲೆ ತಾಂ ಮೋಱ್ ಪೆಱಂ ಗಡಂ ಗಳಮಾದಂ |
ಕೆನ್ನಂ ಸಿಲ್ಲೆಂದಿಪನೆಂ | ದುಂ ನಿಱಿಸಲ್ಕಲ್ಲದೆಡೆಗಳೊಳ್ ಕಲ್ಲದಿರಿಂ ||

We may now consider the several species of composition which Nāgavarma names and defines at the close of his *Kāvyāvalōkana*. He begins with the statement that composition is of three kinds—prose, poetry and both combined, and tells us that a work written in prose is called *Kathā* (or tale) or *Akhyāyika* (or narrative), that when composed in verse and continued in a number of cantos (*Sarga*) it is styled a great poem, and that when written in prose and verse it is termed *Champū*. Again, a piece of poetry, complete in a single stanza, is called *Iḍukungabbam*; where complete in a number of stanzas (usually five), it is known as *Kuḷaka*; and when it consists of a number of independent stanzas, it is termed *Kōsa*. Further, a poem which may extend to twelve stanzas, some of which are in the *kanda* metre interspersed with some in the metre of one of the well-known *vrittas*, is styled *melvāḍu;* that which consists of 15 or 25 stanzas is called *pāḍu;* that which is made up of a number of *pāḍus* is known as *pāḍugabbam*, to which class likewise *melvāḍu* and *bedanḍe-gabbam* belonged; and lastly, that which consists of stanzas composed in a variety of metres is termed *bājane-gabbam*. Of the above, *melvāḍu*, *bedanḍe-gabbam* and *bājane-gabbam*, which are peculiar to Kannaḍa, appear to have been sung with or without the accompaniment of a musical instrument, as is evident from the words *pāḍu* (song) and *bājane* (playing upon a musical instrument). As stated above, Nṛipatuṅga mentions two kinds of composition styled *bedanḍe* and *chattāna*. As Nāgavarma's definition of *bajane-gabbam* nearly agrees with that of *chattāna*, it may be concluded that they are identical. Besides, a comparison of Nāgavarma's definition of *melvāḍu* with that of *bedanḍe* leads one to think that the latter is probably another name for the former. Most of the above kinds of composition have not survived to our times. Among the extant Kannaḍa works, Janna's *Yaśōdharacharita* (1209) is perhaps the only one that seems to answer to the description of *melvāḍu*.

Some of Nāgavarma's observations on poets and poetry deserve notice. Though men may reach the farther shore of the sea of learning, it is only the fortunate among them that become possessors of the world-famed gem of poetical power (v. 425). A poet ought to exercise as great care in the selection and use of words and expressions as a garland-maker in the selection and use of flowers (v. 498).[1] However slight the blemish in the

[1] ಇದು ಸೌಂದರ್ಯಗುಣಪ್ರಕಾಶವಿದು ತಾನಗ್ರಾಮ್ಯತಾಧಾನವಿಂ |
ತಿಮ ಭಾಸ್ವತ್ತ್ವದಭಾಗರಮ್ಯವಿದು ಬಂಧಾಶ್ಲೇಷವಿಚ್ಛಿತ್ತಿಗಾ ||
ಸ್ವದಮೆಂದಿಂತುಚಿತ ಪ್ರಯೋಗವಿಧಿಯಿಂ ಸಯ್ತಪ್ಪಿನಂ ತಿರ್ದ ಪೇ |

body of the woman, poetry, the fame acquired through her will also become sullied, just as a mirror is obscured by a shadow (v. 428). Consequently, he who is desirous of acquiring unsullied fame cannot be too scrupulous in avoiding blemishes in his composition (v. 429).

Verses 55, 65, 209 and 299, which are quoted by Nāgavarma from earlier works, also contain interesting observations on poets and poetry. Verse 55 condemns the combination of Kannaḍa and Sanskrit words in composition, comparing it to the stringing together of pearls and pepper-corns. We have already seen that Nṛipatuṅga compares it to the mixing of drops of butter-milk with boiling milk; Nayasēna (1112) characterises it as a mixing together of clarified butter and oil. According to verse 65, there is as much difference between good and bad poetry as there is between a lute and a wooden stool. Verse 209 states that the heart which is not captivated by elegant poetry is a stony heart which it is impossible even for the arrow of the god of Love to pierce. Verse 299 asks, 'Is he to be reckoned a poet whose obscure effusions require for their comprehension a number of glossaries and commentaries?'

In connection with the simile of a garland-maker to a poet mentioned above, the following observation of Janna is worthy of note:

'Just as a garland, beautifully prepared, must fade in the absence of worthy wearers, even so must a work,

ಬ್ಬಿಪು ಪೂಮಾಲೆಯನಿಂಬಿನಿಂ ಸಮೆವಪೋಲ್ ಸತ್ಕಾವ್ಯಮಂ ಕಬ್ಬಿಗಂ ||

Cp. Nēmichandra:

ಒಟ್ಟೈಗೆ ಬಂದ ಕೋಮಳಗುಣಂ ಗೆಡೆಗೊಂಡಿರೆ ಪೂವಿನಂತಿರಾ |
ಯ್ದಿಟ್ಟ ಪದಂ ಬೆಡಂಗೆಸೆಸೆ ಬಣ್ಣಸರಂ ಪೊಸತಾಗೆ ನುಣ್ಪುಡಂ ||
ಬಟ್ಟರೆ ಬಂಧಮೊಂದೆ ಚತುರಾಳಿ ಕರಂ ಬಸಮಾಗೆ ಬಾಸಿಗಂ |
ಗಟ್ಟುವನಂತೆ ಕಟ್ಟುವುದು ಕಬ್ಬಮನುಬ್ಬಣಮಾಗೆ ಕಬ್ಬಿಗಂ ||

Cp. also Bhāmaha:

ಏತದ್ಗ್ರಾಹ್ಯಂ ಸುರಭಿಕುಸುಮಂ ಗ್ರಾಮ್ಯಮೇತನ್ನಧೇಯಂ |
ಧತ್ತೇ ಶೋಭಾಂ ವಿರಚಿತಮಿದಂ ಸ್ಥಾನಮಸ್ಯೈತದಸ್ಯ ||
ಮಾಲಾಕಾರೋ ರಚಯತಿ ಯಥಾ ಸಾಧು ವಿಜ್ಞಾಯ ಮಾಲಾಂ |
ಯೋಜ್ಯಂ ಕಾವ್ಯೇಷ್ವವಹಿತಧಿಯಾ ತದ್ವದೇವಾಭಿಧಾನಂ ||

(*Kāvyālankāra*, I, 59).

excellently composed, prove useless in the absence of worthy scholars to appreciate it.'[1]

A few words may be said here about the Poetical conventions (Kavi-samaya) dealt with in four sections in the fifth chapter of *Kāvyāvalōkana*. The first section treats of those conceits which, though they have no foundation in fact, are still embodied in poetry as if they were true, e.g., the Chakōra bird drinking the moonlight, lotuses growing in rivers, swans and other birds haunting all receptacles of water. The second section deals with those things which, though they undoubtedly exist, are considered as non-existent for practical purposes, e.g., the fruit in the Aśōka tree, the Jāti flower in spring, the blooming of lilies during the day. The third section speaks of the limitation with regard to time or place which the convention of the poet imposes upon certain things, though no such limitation exists in nature. For example, the sandal tree is described as growing only in the Malaya Mountain; and the cuckoo is supposed to cry only in spring. The last section refers to the identity assumed by poets between things which are different from each other. For instance, identity is assumed between the hare and the antelope in the description of the moon's spot; and between the fish and the *makara* in describing the crest of the God of Love.

A great poem has to treat of the following 18 subjects, which are styled its *angas* or limbs or constituents:

ಉದಧಿ ಪುರಾಧಿಪ ಸುತ ಮಂ | ತ್ರ ದೂತ ಗಮನಾಜಿ ವಿರಹ ಪರಿಣಯ ಸುರತ |
ರ್ತು ದಿನೇಶ ಚಂದ್ರ ಮಧು ಪುಷ್ಪ | ದುದಕ ವನಸ್ಪತಿಯೆ ಕೃತಿಗೆ ಪದಿನೆಂಟಂಗಂ ||

(*Udayādityālankāra*).

The following verse which states the subjects more

[1] ಎನಿತನೊಳಿಲ್ದು ಪೇಳ್ದ ಕವಿಯೋವನದಂ ಪೆಸರಿಟ್ಟು ಮೆಚ್ಚಬ |
ಲ್ಲನನಱಿಸಲ್ಕೆ ವೇಳ್ದುದವನಂ ಜಗದೊಳ್ ಪಡೆಯಲ್ಕೆ ಬಾರದಾ ||
ತನ ಮುಖದಿಂದಮಲ್ಲದದು ಸಲ್ಲದು ಕಟ್ಟಿಯುಮೇನೊ ಮಾಲೆಗಾ |
ಱನ ಪೊಸಬಾಸಿಗಂ ಮುಡಿವ ಭೋಗಿಗಳಿಲ್ಲದೆ ಬಾಡಿಪೋಗದೇ ||

Cp. ಪರಿಹೇಶರಿ ನಷ್ಟಲೋಚನೇ ಸಫಲಃ ಕಿಂನು ಕಳತ್ರವಿಭ್ರಮಃ ||
Cp. also ಆಪರಿತೋಷಾದ್ವಿದುಷಾಂ ನ ಸಾಧು ಮನ್ಯೇ ಪ್ರಯೋಗವಿಜ್ಞಾನಂ ||

clearly is taken from Mallikārjuna's *Sūktisudhārṇava*, an anthology consisting of verses from earlier poets relating to each one of the above mentioned 18 *angas*.

ವಾರಿಧಿ ಪರ್ವತಂ ಪುರಮಧೀಶ್ವರನುದ್ವಹನಂ ಕುಮಾರನಂ |
ಘೋರುಹವೈರಿಮಿತ್ರರುದಯಂ ಋತು ನಂದನಮಂಬು ಸೀದು ಕಾಂ ||
ತಾರತಿ ಚಿಂತೆ ಮಂತ್ರ ಚರ ಯಾನ ವಿರೋಧಿಜಯಂಗಳೆಂಬಿವಂ |
ಸೂರಿಗಳಂಗಮೆಂದು ಕೃತಿಯೊಳ್ ಪದಿನೆಂಟುಮನೆಯ್ದೆ ಬಣ್ಣಿಪರ್ ||

The sea, mountain, city, king, marriage, prince, sunrise, moonrise, seasons, pleasure-garden, sport in water, drinking, amorous intercourse, separation from the beloved, deliberation, messenger, journey and defeat of the enemy.

The terms *mārga* and *dēsi* frequently occur in Kannaḍa literature. They seem to indicate Sanskrit and vernacular usages respectively as may be inferred from the following stanzas from *Saṅgītaratnākara*:

ಗೀತಂ ವಾದ್ಯಂ ತಥಾ ನೃತ್ತಂ ತ್ರಯಂ ಸಂಗೀತಮುಚ್ಯತೇ |
ಮಾರ್ಗೋ ದೇಶೀತಿ ತದ್ದ್ವೇಧಾ ತತ್ರ ಮಾರ್ಗಸ್ಸ ಉಚ್ಯತೇ ||
ಯೋ ಮಾರ್ಗಿತೋ ವಿರಿಂಚಾದ್ಯೈಃ ಪ್ರಯುಕ್ತೋ ಭರತಾದಿಭಿಃ |
ದೇವಸ್ಯ ಪುರತಶ್ಶಂಭೋರ್ನಿಯತೋಽಭ್ಯುದಯಪ್ರದಃ |
ದೇಶೇ ದೇಶೇ ಜನಾನಾಂ ಯದ್ರುಚ್ಯಾ ಹೃದಯರಂಜಕಂ |
ಗೀತಂ ಚ ವಾದನಂ ನೃತ್ತಂ ತದ್ದೇಶೀತ್ಯಭಿಧೀಯತೇ ||

I may close this section by giving the peculiar characteristics of the Kannaḍa Language as stated by Keśirāja in his *Śabdamaṇidarpaṇa*. He says:

Is not Kannaḍa difficult by reason of its Gamaka-compounds, its distinction between ಱ, ೞ, and the Sanskrit ಲ or ೞ, its agreeable euphony, its appropriate use of the locative-infinitive, its employment of words common to Sanskrit and Kannaḍa, its distinction between *va* and *ma* and *ha* and *pa*, its use of Sanskrit themes excluding particles, its fleeting consonants, and its violation of *yati* or pause in verses?[1]

[1] ಗಮಕಸಮಾಸದಿಂ ಱಳಕುಳಕ್ಷಳದಿಂ ಶ್ರುತಿಸಹ್ಯಸಂಧಿಯಿಂ |
ಸಮುಚಿತಮಾಗಿ ಬರ್ಪ ಸತಿಸಪ್ತಮಿಯಿಂ ಸಮಸಂಸ್ಕೃತೋಕ್ತಿಯಿಂ ||
ವಮಹಪಭೇದದಿಂ ವಿರಹಿತಾವ್ಯಯಸಂಸ್ಕೃತಲಿಂಗದಿಂ ಪದೋ|
ತ್ತನುಶಿಥಿಲತ್ವದಿಂ ಯತಿವಿಲಂಘನದಿಂದರಿದಲ್ತೆ ಕನ್ನಡಂ ||

Classes of Poets

Kannaḍa poets may be roughly classed as Jainas, Vīraśaivas and Brāhmaṇas. There are also authors of other sects, but their number is comparatively small. The earliest cultivators of the language for literary purposes were the Jainas and down to the 12th century, we have, with very few exceptions, only Jaina authors. For about three centuries after that period, we have along with them a few Brāhmaṇa writers and a pretty large number of Vīraśaiva authors, and from about the 15th century date numerous Brāhmanical and Vīraśaiva works. There were, however, during these later periods, some compositions by the Jainas, but most of the literature of later times originated with the other sects. The leading characteristic of the Jaina earlier works is that they are *champū-kāvyas* or poems in a variety of composite metres interspersed with paragraphs in prose. The Jainas also wrote particular compositions such as *chattāna*, *bedanḍe* and *melvāḍu* which have not come down to us. In Jaina works of a later period the *sāngatya* and *shaṭpadi* metres are largely used as in Brāhmanical and Vīraśaiva works. The earlier Vīraśaiva works are mostly in the form of *vachanas* or poetical prose, and occasionally in the *ragaḷe* and *tripadi* metres. The *vachanas* are written in simple, lucid, vigorous prose with the object of popularising religious and philosophical truths. The most recent compositions of all the sects are mostly in the form of *Yakshagānas* or rustic dramas interspersed with songs, and some in prose only. There were also some female authors in all the sects.

A Bird's-Eye View of Kannaḍa Literature

We shall now take a bird's-eye view of Kannaḍa literature century by century, from the 9th to the 18th.

Authors of the 9th Century

We have already spoken of Nṛipatuṅga as the author of *Kavirājamārga*. He evidently took a great interest in the Kannaḍa country, people and language. Of the poets named by him, Srīvijaya, who is mentioned as the author of *Chandraprabha-purāṇa* by Mangarasa III and Doḍḍaiya and highly praised by Durgasimha (c. 1025)[1], and who appears to be named in *Kavirājamārga* itself, may belong to the early part of this century. Gunavarma I, the author of *Śūdraka*, *Harivamśa* and other works which are quoted from by later writers, was patronised by the Ganga King Eṟeyappa (886–913) whom he has identified with the ancient King Śūdraka in his work of that name.

Authors of the 10th Century

It is not possible to do more than briefly name some of the principal Kannaḍa authors who followed and their chief works, with dates where they are known. Pampa I, deservedly regarded as the greatest of Kannaḍa poets, wrote *Ādipurāṇa* and *Vikramārjunavijaya* in 941. The latter work is also known as *Pampa-Bhārata* in which the author has identified his patron, a Chāḷukya prince named Arikēsari, with Arjuna and made him the hero. He states that his *Bhārata* and *Ādipurāṇa* put all former poems under their feet and that he completed the one in six months and the other in three months. He was the descendant of a Jaina from the Veṅgi country. Ponna, who wrote *Śāntipurāṇa*, claims to be superior to all other poets in command of both Kannaḍa and Sanskrit. He received the title, Kavichakravarti, from the Rāshtra-kūta King Krishṇa III (939–68). In 978, we have Chāvuṇḍaraya, the author of *Chāvuṇḍarāya-purāṇa*, an excellent specimen of prose composition of that period. It gives an account of the 24 Tīrthankaras. Next came Ranna, the author of *Ajitapurāṇa* (993) and of *Sāhasa-bhīmavijaya*, also known as *Gadāyuddha*, the hero of which is the Chāḷukya prince Satyāśraya. Ranna received the title Kavichakravarti from the Chāḷukya King Tailapa (973–97). At the same time as the two preceding we have Nāgavarma I, who was the author of *Chhandōmbudhi*, the first work extant on prosody, and probably also of *Kādambari*, a close metrical version of Bāṇa's Sanskrit

[1] ಶ್ರೀವಿಜಯರ ಕವಿಮಾರ್ಗಂ | ಭಾವಿಪ ಕವಿಜನದ ಮನಕೆ ಕನ್ನಡಿಯುಂ ಕೈ | ಯ್ದೀವಿಗೆಯುಮಾದುದು.

work. To the close of the same century may be assigned Gajānkuśa, Manasija and Chandrabhatta, who, though their works have not come down to us, are honorably mentioned as eminent poets by later writers. All the authors mentioned were Jainas.

Authors of the 11th Century

In the 11th century have to be placed Srīdharāchārya, who wrote *Jātakatilaka*, the first work on astrology in the language, in 1049, during the rule of the Chāḷukya King Āhavamalla or Trailōkyamalla (1042–68); and Śāntinātha, who completed his poem *Sukumāracharita* in 1068 during the reign of the Chāḷukya King Bhuvanaikamalla (1068–76). These two were Jaina poets. Among the Brāhman authors of the century may be mentioned Durgasimha, the author of *Panchatantra*, who was the minister for peace and war of the Chāḷukya King Jayasimha-Jagadēkamalla I (1018–42); and Chandrarāja, who wrote *Madanatilaka*, under the patronage of Māchirāja, a feudatory of the same king. Chandrarāja seems to have been a versatile scholar who wrote on a variety of subjects. There are not many names in this century, owing probably to the check caused by the Chōḷa invasions.

Authors of the 12th Century

The 12th century, when Mysore was restored to Kannaḍa rule under the Hoysaḷas, seems to have been specially prolific in Kannaḍa works of high excellence. Nāgachandra or Abhinava-Pampa, author of *Rāmachandracharitapurāṇa*, also known as *Pampa Rāmāyaṇa*, and of *Mallinātha-purāṇa;* Rājāditya, author of *Vyavahāragaṇita* and other mathematical works; Kīrtivarma, a Chāḷukya prince, author of *Gōvaidya*, the earliest veterinary work in the language; Nagavarma II, the Kaṭakācharya (poet-laureate) of the Chāḷukya king Jagadēkamalla II and author of several important works on the language, namely, *Kāvyāvalōkana*, a comprehensive work on poetics, *Karṇāṭaka-Bhāshābhūshaṇa*, a grammar in Sanskrit sutras, and *Vastukōśa*, lexicon giving Kannaḍa equivalents of Sanskrit words; Jagaddaḷasōmanātha, author of the medical work *Karṇāṭaka-Kalyāṇakāraka*, the earliest work on medicine; Nēmichandra, author of a romance called *Līlāvati* and a Purāṇa named *Ardhanēmi* from its being only half-finished; and Aggaḷa, author of *Chandraprabha-purāṇa*—were all Jainas, as well as the poetess Kanti.

Among writers of other faiths at this time, may be mentioned the Brāhmaṇa poets Rudrabhatta, author of *Jagannātha-vijaya*, who wrote under the patronage of Chandramauli, minister of the Hoysaḷa King Ballāḷa II, Kāma, author of *Sriṅgāra-ratnākāra*, a work on poetics; and Dēva, author of the romance *Kusumāvaḷi*. The Chōla Prince Udayāditya, author of a small work on rhetoric named after him, also comes here. Among the Vīraśaiva writers of this century are Basava, Chennabasava, Prabhudēva, Siddharāma, Koṇḍagūḷi-Kēśirāja and a host of others including a pretty large number of women, who have mostly written *vachanas;* Harīśvara, author of *Girijā-kalyāṇa* and other works; Rāghavāṅka, his nephew, author of *Hariśchandra-Kāvya* and other works in the *shaṭpadi* metre; Keṛeya-Padmarasa, author of *Dīkshā-bōdhe* in the *ragaḷe* metre; and Pālkurike-Sōmanātha, author of *Sīlasampādane* and other works, who has also written in Telugu.

Authors of the 13th Century

In the 13th century, we find a group of excellent Jaina poets, all closely related to one another, patronised by the Hoysaḷa kings. Janna, author of *Yaśōdhara-charita* (1209) and *Anantanāthapurāṇa* (1230), who received the title Kavichakravarti from Ballāḷa II, was the son of Sumanōbāṇa, the poet-laureate of Narasimha II; his sister's husband, Mallikārjuna, wrote the anthology *Sūkti-sudhārṇava* for the recreation of King Sōmēśvara; and his son, Kēśirāja, was the author of the standard Kannaḍa grammar *Sabdamaṇidarpaṇa*. Other Jaina poets of this period were Pārśva-panḍita, author of *Pārśvanāthapurāṇa*; Guṇavarma II, author of *Pushpadanta-purāṇa*; Aṇḍayya, author of *Kabbigara-kāva*, a work of special interest from its being written in pure Kannaḍa without the admixture of Sanskrit words as such, though *tadbhavas* are largely used;[1] Kumudēndu, author of *Kumudēndu-Rāmāyaṇa* in the *shaṭpadi* metre; Raṭṭakavi, author of *Raṭṭamata*, a work on meteorology and omens; and Śiśu-Māyaṇa, author of *Tripura-dahana* and *Anjanā-charite*, works written for the first time in the *sāngatya* metre, intended to be sung to the accompaniment of some musical instrument.

Of other writers of this period may be named Polāḷ-vadaṇḍanātha, author of *Hari-charitra*, who was successively the minister of Ballāḷa II and Narasimha II, and built the Harihareśvara temple at Harihar (1224); and Chauṇḍarasa, author of *Abhinava-Daśakumāra-charite*, a metrical version of Daṇḍi's Sanskrit work, *Nalacharite* and other works. The only Vīraśaiva writer of importance in this century was Sōmarāja, author of *Udbhaṭakāvya* (1222).

Authors of the 14th Century

The 14th century produced, among others, the Jaina poets Nāgarāja, author of *Punyāsrava* (1331); Bāhubali-paṇḍita, author of *Dharmanātha-purāṇa* (1352); Mangarāja I, author of *Khagēndramaṇidarpaṇa*, a work on taxicology; Madhura, author of *Dharmanātha-purāṇa*, who was patronised by Mudda-daṇḍanatha, minister of Harihara II and Lakshmīdhara, minister of Dēvarāya I; and Vrittavilāsa, author of *Dharmaparīkshe* and *Śāstra-sāra*; the Brāhmaṇa poets, Mangarāja II; author of *Mangarāja-nighanṭu* (1398), a metrical lexicon giving Kannaḍa meanings of Sanskrit words; Abhinava-Chandra, author of the veterinary work *Aśva-vaidya*; Kavi Malla, author of *Manmathavijaya*; and the Vīraśaiva poets Bhīmakavi, author of *Basava-purāṇa* (1969) and Padmaṇānka, author of *Padmarāja-purāṇa*.

Authors of the 15th Century

From the 15th century, the authors become too numerous to allow of more than a few of the principal

[1] Cp. the Telugu *Yayaticharitre* of the sixteenth century by Ponnaganti Teluganna and the *Achcha-Tenugu Rāmāyaṇa* of the 18th century by Kuchimanchi Timmakavi.

ones being named. Among the Jaina poets, who are rarely met with from this century onwards, may be mentioned as belonging to this time, Bhāskara, author of *Jīvandhara-charite* (1424); Kalyāṇakīrti, author of *Jnāna-chandrābhyudaya* (1439); Vijayaṇṇa, author of *Dvādaśānuprēkshe* (1448); Bommarasa of Terakanāmbi, author of *Sanatkumāracharite*; and Srīdharadēva, author of the medical work, *Vaidyāmṛita*. Among the Brāhmans were Kumāra-Vyāsa, author of *Karṇāta-Bhārata*; Kumāra-Vālmiki, author of *Torave-Rāmāyaṇa*; Mādhava, author of *Mādhavālankāra*; a translation of Daṇḍi's *Kāvyādarśa*; and Īśvara-kavi, also known as Bāṇa-kavi, author of *Kavijihvā-bandhana*, a work on prosody.

Among the Vīraśaiva poets may be named Dēparāja, author of a collection of romances called *Sobagina-sōne*; Chāmarasa, author of *Prabhulingalīle*; Guru-Basava, author of *Śivayogānga-bhūshaṇa* and other works; Chandra-kavi; author of *Virūpakshāsthāna*; Bommarasa, author of *Saundara-purāṇa*; Kallarasa, author of *Jana-vaśya*, also called *Madanatilaka*; Nīlakaṇṭhāchārya, author of *Ārādhya-charitra*; Chaturmukha-Bommarasa, author of *Rēvaṇasiddhēsvara-purāṇa*; Singirāja, author of *Mala-basavarāja-charitra*; Nijaguṇa-Śivayōgi, author of *Anubhavasāra* and other works; and Suranga-kavi, author of *Triśashṭi-purātanara-Charitre*, giving an account of the sixty-three devotees of Śiva.

Authors of the 16th Century

The 16th century saw a prolific production of works of the Vīraśaivas, though authors of other sects were not idle. Among the Vīraśaivas were Mallaṇārya of Gubbi, author of *Bhāvachintāratna* (1513) and *Vīra-śaivāmṛitapurāṇa* (1530); Nanjuṇḍa, author of *Kumāra-rāma-charite;* Chēramānka, author of *Chēramakāvya*; Lingamantri, author of the lexicon, *Kabbigarakaipiḍi;* Vīrabhadrarāja, author of *Vīrabhadra-vijaya* and other works; Chennabasavānka, author of *Mahādēviyakkana-purāṇa;* Nanjuṇḍa of Kikkēri, author of *Bhairavēśvara-Kāvya*; Sadāsiva-Yōgi, author of *Rāmanātha-vilāsa*; Virakta Tonṭadārya, author of *Siddhēsvara-purāṇa*, the lexicon *Karṇāṭakaśabdamañjari* and other works; and Virūpākshapaṇḍita (1584), author of *Chennabasvapurāṇa*.

Among the Jainas were Maṅgarasa III, author of *Jayanṛipa-kāvya* and other works; Abhinava-Vādividyānanda, author of the anthology *Kāvyasāra*; Sālva, author of *Bhārata*, *Rasaratnākara* and other works; Ratnākaravarṇi, author of *Bharatesvara Charite* and other works; Dēvōttama, author of the lexicon, *Nanārtharatnākara*; and Śāntarasa, author of *Yōgaratnākara*; and among Brāhmaṇas, Timmaṇṇa-kavi, author of the latter portion of *Bhārata*; Sadānanda-yōgi, author of portions of *Bhāgavata* and *Bhārata*; Purandaradāsa, author of numerous songs in praise of Vishṇu; Tirumala-Bhatta, author of *Śiva-gīte*; and Timma, author of *Navarasālankāra*; among others Rāmēndra, author of *Saundarya-Kathāratna*, a metrical version in the *iripadi* metre of *Battīsaputtaḷikathe*; and Kanakadasa, author of *Mōhanatarangiṇi* and other works as well as songs.

Authors of the 17th Century

In the 17th century the literary output of the Brāhmaṇas was greater than that of the writers of other religious denominations. A remarkable development of Kannaḍa literature also took place in the latter part of the century during the rule of Chikkadēvarāja Oḍeyar (1672–1704), one of the most distinguished kings of Mysore, who was not only a great patron of literary merit, but also an author himself. Two of the ministers, Tirumalārya and Chikkupādhyāya, have not only written works of great excellence but have also encouraged others to write good works. Among Tirumalārya's works may be mentioned *Apratimavīra-charite*, a rhetorical work in praise of the king, *Chikkadēvarāja-vijaya*, a *Champū* work describing the king's conquests, and *Chikkadēvarāja-vamśāvaḷi*, a prose work giving an account of the king's ancestors. Chikkupādhyāya may be said to be the most voluminous writer in Kannaḍa, his works being more than thirty in number. Among the more important were *Vishṇu-purāṇa* (1691), *Kamalāchaḷamāhātmya* (1680), *Hastigiri-māhātmya* (1679), *Rukmāngada-*

charite (1681) and *Sātvikabrahmavidyāvilāsa*, a work on Viśishtādvaita philosophy. Singarārya, brother of Tirumalārya, wrote a drama called *Mitravindāgōvinda*. Among other poets that were patronised by the king or his ministers were Timmakavi, author of *Yādavagiri-māhātmya* (1677) and other works; Mallikārjuna, author of *Srīranga-māhātmya* (1678); Mallarasa, author of *Daśāvatāra Charite*, and the poetess, Srīrangamma, who wrote *Padminī Kalyāṇa*. There was likewise at the court an Okkaliga poetess, Honnamma, who composed *Hadibadeya Dharma*, a work on the duties of a faithful wife. Among the remaining Brāhmaṇa poets of this century were Rāmachandra, author of *Aśvaśāstra*; Tirumalevaidya, author of *Uttara Rāmāyaṇa*; Nāgarasa, author of *Bhagavadgīte*; Timmarasa, author of *Kshētra-gaṇita* or Geometry and Lakshmīśa author of *Jaimini Bhārata*, which is probably the most popular poem in the language.

Among the Jainas were Bhāttakaḷanka, author of *Karṇāṭaka Śabdānuśāsana* (1604), an exhaustive grammar of the language in Sanskrit sūtras, with an extensive Sanskrit commentary; Padmana-paṇḍita, author of *Hayasāra-samuchchaya*; Chidānanda, author of *Munivamśābhyu-daya*; and Chandrasēkhara, author of *Rāmachandra-charitra*. The Vīraśaiva poets of note of the century were Harīśvara, author of *Prabhudēva-purāṇa*; Siddhanañjēsa, author of *Rāghavāṅka-Charitra* and *Gururāja Charitra*; Pemmisetti or Prāsabhūshaṇa, author of *Gurubhaktāṇḍāra Charitre*; Mummaḍi Tamma, author of *Śankara Samhita*; Parvatēśvara, author of *Chaturā-chāryapurāṇa*; Shadaksharadēva, author of *Rājaśekhara-Vilāsa* (1655), a poem which appears to divide with the *Jaimini Bhārata* the honour of being the most popular work in Kannaḍa, *Vṛishabhēndra-vijaya* and *Śabara-śankara-vilāsa*; and Sejjeya Siddhalingārya, author of *Malayarāja-charite*. Sarvajña, author of the popular *tripadi* verses going by his name, may also be assigned to this century.

Authors of the 18th Century

The 18th century witnessed the rise of a popular kind of literature, Yakshagānas, though there is evidence to show that one or two of them were written in the latter part of the previous century. These are opera pieces or rude forms of dramatic representation suited to rustic audiences. As a rule, they are characterised neither by dramatic skill nor by literary merit. The works are mostly based on some incident or other of that inexhaustible store-house of old stories, the Purāṇas, and are generally acted in villages to the immense joy of the masses. It is not to be understood that there were no other kinds of literature during this period, though the number of Jaina and Vīraśaiva authors of any merit was very small. Among the Brāhmaṇa writers were Lakshmakavi, author of *Bhārata* and *Rukmāngada-charite;* Venkaṭeśa, author of the Champu work, *Hālāsya-māhātmya;* Kōnayya, author of *Krishṇārjuna Sangara;* Timmāmātya, author of a Rāmāyaṇa called *Rāmābhyudaya-Kathākusumamañjari*; Bālavaidyada Cheluva, author of Kannaḍa *Līlāvati* and *Ratnaśāstra*, a treatise on precious stones; and the poetess, Heḷavanakatte Giriyamma, who wrote *Chandrahasanakathe* and other works.

Among the Vīraśaivas may be mentioned Sankarakavi, author of *Chōrabasava-charitre* and Nūronda, author of *Saundara-kāvya:* among the Jainas, Pāyaṇṇa, author of *Ahimsācharite,* Padmarāja, author of *Pūjyapāda-charite* (1792); Padmanābha, author of *Rāmachandra-charitre;* and Surāḷa, author of *Padmāvati-charitre*; and among others Kaḷale-Nanjarāja, author of *Kakudgiri-māhātmya* and other works; Jayēndra, author of *Karṇāṭaka-Kuvalayānanda*; and the poetess Cheluvāmbe, Queen of the Mysore King, Krishṇaraja Oḍeyar I, who composed *Varanandīkalyāṇa* and other works. The century was also remarkable for the number of popular devotional songs known as *Dāsara-padagaḷu* composed by devotees of Vishṇu, especially of the Mādhava sect.

The Modern Period

In the 19th century, a great impetus was given to the advancement of Kannaḍa literature during the rule of the Mysore King, Krishṇaraja Oḍeyar III, who was a munificent patron of all kinds of literary merit and afforded special encouragement to the production of Kannaḍa versions of all the more important Sanskrit works. He was himself a voluminous writer, about forty Kannaḍa works being attributed to him, of which may be mentioned a poetical romance named *Saugandhikā-pariṇaya*. Under his patronage, the number of *Yaksha-gānas* increased and gained popularity. Aḷīya-Liṅgarāja has written nearly thirty Yakshagānas besides a few poems, such as the *Prabhāvatīpariṇaya*, which are of considerable literary merit. The Jaina author, Dēvachandra, wrote in 1838 the *Rajāvaḷikathe*, a cyclopædia of Jaina traditional history and chronology, at the instance of Devīrammaṇṇi, a Queen of the Mysore Royal Family. Chandrasāgara-varṇi, author of the *Kadambapurāṇa* and other works, was a voluminous Jaina writer. The last quarter of the century may be said to have witnessed a revival of Kannaḍa learning. Under the late Chāmarājēndra Oḍeyar of Mysore, encouragement was given to the production of dramatic works of a high order, which were put on the stage. Educated men have begun in earnest to enrich Kannaḍa literature by writing original works, translations or adaptations. Among modern poets who have made valuable additions to the stock of works in the language may be mentioned Basappa Śāstri, S. G. Narasimhā-chārya, Nandaḷige Lakshmīnāranappa, Dhōnḍo Nara-simha Mulabāgilu and Śānta Kavi or Bālāchārya Sakkari. B. Venkaṭāchārya has added many useful prose works to Kannaḍa literature which afford healthy reading to the public.

This survey of Kannaḍa literature, though necessarily brief, is enough to bring to view its vast extent which does not at all compare unfavourably with that of any other vernacular of the South.

CHAPTER III

CONNECTION OF KANNAḌA LITERATURE WITH THOSE OF TELUGU, TAMIL AND SANSKRIT

Connection of Kannaḍa and Telugu Literatures

THE connection between Kannaḍa and Telugu literatures appears to be much closer than that between Kannaḍa and Tamil literatures. One of the reasons for this may be that the Chāḷukyas ruled over both the Karṇāta and Āndhra countries and patronised both the languages. Several Telugu authors have also written in Kannaḍa and vice versa. The metre *Akkara* which seems to be peculiar to Kannaḍa is found in early Telugu works and inscriptions such as Nannayya-Bhatta's *Bhārata* and the Bezwāḍa Pillar inscription of Yuddhamalla. Two of the early Kannaḍa poets, viz., Pampa I (941) and Nāgavarma I (c. 990) were descendants of men who belonged to Vengimaṇḍala. We learn from an inscription which records the grant of a village in 1053 by the Eastern Chāḷukya King Rājarāja to Nārāyaṇa-Bhaṭṭa, who helped Nannayya-Bhaṭṭa in the composition of the Telugu *Bhārata*, that Nārāyaṇa-Bhaṭṭa was also a Kannaḍa poet.[1] Pālkurike Sōmanātha and Vēmulavāḍa Bhīma-Kavi, who were great Telugu poets, have written Kannaḍa works also: the former *Śīlasampādane*, etc., and the latter, *Basavapurāṇa*. Piduparti Sōmanātha has translated into Telugu the Kannaḍa *Prabhulingalīle* of Chāmaraśa. The fact of the matter is that Telugu scholars of that period were also well-versed in Sanskrit and Kannaḍa and it is on account of this familiarity with Kannaḍa that the poet Srinatha describes his Telugu as Kannaḍa.[2] He calls

[1] ಯಃ ಸಂಸ್ಕೃತ ಕರ್ಣಾಟ ಪ್ರಾಕೃತ ಪೈಶಾಚಕಾಂಧ್ರಭಾಷಾಸು |
ಕವಿರಾಜಶೇಖರ ಇತಿ ಪ್ರಥಿತಃ ಸುಕವಿತ್ವವಿಭವೇನ ||

[2] ಪ್ರೌಢಿಂಬಲಿಕಿಂಪ ಸಂಸ್ಕೃತ ಭಾಷಯಂಡ್ರು | ಪಲುಕು ನುಡಿಕಾರಮುನನಾಂಧ್ರಭಾಷ
ಯಂದು | ರೆವ್ವರೇಮನ್ನನಂಡ್ರು ನಾಕೇಲ ಕೊಱತ | ನಾ ಕವಿತ್ವಂಬು ನಿಜಮು ಕರ್ಣಾಟಭಾಷ ||

himself Karṇāṭadēśakaṭaka-padmavana-kēli. Nannechōḍa, Piduparti Basava, Dhūrjaṭi, and other Telugu poets knew Kannaḍa also, as can be inferred from their works. In his *Śṛingāra Naishadha*, Srīnātha applies the Kannaḍa title Svāmidrōharaganḍa to the minister Nāmāmātya. Nannechōḍa (c. 1150) uses in his *Kumārasambhava* several Kannaḍa words. He was a Chōḷa Chief, son of Chōḷaballi, perhaps identical with Mallidēva Chōḷa named in Challakere 43, of 1108, and Challakere 21, of 1147. The Kannaḍa words used by him are *Nāyi* (dog), *dēsi* (beauty),[1] *venchalu* (pond, cp. *bench*?) and *Kolavēlu* for *Kolavēr* (cuscus grass).[2] The chief Baddena (c. 1260), who wrote *Nītiśāstramuktāvali*, had the Kannaḍa title *Aṇṇanagandhavāraṇa*.

Of the Kannaḍa poets who were also Telugu scholars or authors may be mentioned Nīlakaṇṭhāchārya (c. 1485), who has translated into Kannaḍa *Shaṭpadi*, the Telugu *Paṇḍitārādhyacharite* in *dvipadi* of Pālkurike Sōmanātha; Pemmisetti (c. 1650), who has likewise translated the Telugu *Gurubhaktāṇḍāra Charite* in *dvipadi* of Pālkurike Sōmānatha into Kannaḍa *shaṭpadi*; Chakrapāṇi Ranganātha (c. 1195), who wrote *Srīgirināthavikrama* in Telugu; Tirumalabhaṭṭa (c. 1600), whose metrical translation of *Śivagīte* is based on Harihārāradhya's Telugu commentary on the work; and Mummaḍi Tamma (c. 1665), a chief of Sugaṭur who wrote the Telugu works *Rājēndrachōḷacharite*, *Kumārārjunīya*, *Saundarēśacharite*. There are, further, Hubbaḷḷi Sangayya (c. 1700), Vīrarāja (c. 1720), Kaḷale Nanjarāja (c.1740) and Śālyada Krishnarāja, among others, who were likewise Telugu scholars. Among modern authors may be named Venkaṭaramaṇaiya (1857), who wrote *Gayōpakhyāna* in Kannaḍa and *Adhyātma-Rāmāyāṇa* in Telugu.

[1] ಭಾಸುರಾಂಗಮುಲಿಂತ ದೇಸಿಯಗುನೇ.

[2] It is ವಟ್ಟಿವೇಳ್ಳು in Telugu. Mr. Vīrēśalingam Pantalu took *Kaṇḍavaḍam* used by Nannechōda also for a Kannaḍa word, but it is a *tadbhava* of the Sanskrit Kāṇḍapaṭa.

Connection of Kannaḍa and Tamil Literatures

Such interchanges between Kannaḍa and Tamil literatures are, however, very few. Amṛitasāgara, a Jaina Tamil poet, who flourished before the 11th century, states in his *Yāpparuṅgalakkārigai*, a work on prosody, that there existed in the Kannaḍa Language a work on prosody named *Guṇa-gānkiyam* and that the Tamil work adopted some of its characteristics, one of which was addressing the rules to a woman.[1] Unfortunately, the name of the author is not given, nor has the work come down to us. It is very probable that this author dedicated his work to the Eastern Chāḷukya King, Vijayāditya III (844-88), who had the distinctive epithets, Guṇaga, Guṇagānka, and Guṇakenalla. This would be the earliest work on prosody in Kannaḍa. Mallaṇārya of Gubbi (1513) says that his poem *Bhāvachintāratna* is a Kannaḍa rendering of the Tamil account of King Satyēndrachōḷa, narrated by Tirujñānasambandha to Kulachcharaiya after confuting Jainism. And Śivaprakāśasvāmi of the 17th century has written metrical translations of the Kannaḍa works, the *Prabhulingalīle* of Chāmarasa and the *Vivēkachintāmaṇi* (only the *Vēdānta-parichchēda*) of Nijaguṇaśivayōgi. The latter version is styled *Vēdāntachūḷāmaṇi*.

It may be added here that every one of the South-Indian languages has numerous translations of Sanskrit works. In Kannaḍa the Jainas and Brāhmaṇas have translated more Sanskrit works than the Vīraśaivas. This can be verified by a mere glance at the list of works given in the volumes of the *Karṇātaka Kavicharite*. In these circumstances it is interesting to note some instances of Kannaḍa works having been translated into Sanskrit.

Nirvāṇa-Mantri (c. 1725), the minister of the Keḷadi chief, Sōmaśēkhara Nāyaka (1714-39), translated into Sanskrit portions of Nijaguṇaśivayōgi's *Vivēkachintāmaṇi*; and Srīmat-Paramahaṁsa Bālakṛishna Brahmānanda-Rājayōgi translated into Sanskrit Ranganātha's *Anubhavāmṛita* in 1813.

[1] ಗುಣಗಾಂಕಿಯಮೆನ್ನುಂ ಕರುನಾಟಕಚ್ಚಂದಮೇಪೋಲ್ ಮಗಡೂಉಮುನ್ನಿಲೈ ಯುಡೈತ್ತಾಯ್ ಅವ್ವೈಯುದಕ್ಕಮುಡೈತ್ತಾಯ್ |

Criticisms

It gives me much pleasure to see that several scholars have now begun to take interest in Kannaḍa literature, though at the time when I began to write the *Kavicharite* there were very few people interested in the study of this subject. I am also glad to see in journals and newspapers criticisms made by some scholars with regard to my work. In a work of this magnitude, involving a great deal of study and investigation, it is but natural that there should be found mistakes here and there; and I shall only be too grateful to scholars who help me in rectifying them and thus making the work more useful. Of these critics, Dr. A. Venkatasubbaiya, M.A., Ph.D., LL.B., has to be given the first place as he has paid the greatest possible attention to my work, especially the first volume, his criticisms extending over nearly 280 printed pages. These criticisms are published in the issues of the *Prabuddha Karṇātaka*. They have also been collected together and issued in the form of a book. Some of the Doctor's criticisms, such as those relating to the age of the poets, Durgasimha, Chandrarāja, Rājāditya and Vrittavilāsa, as also those regarding my identification of some Jaina gurus, are perfectly reasonable. There are others, however, which are based on very weak grounds due to a misunderstanding of the points at issue, while there are others still which, I am constrained to say, are nothing but the outcome of a prejudiced mentality solely intent on fault-finding. Though many of the criticisms are not thus of much value, I have still to thank the Doctor for having given me an opportunity of re-examining my position. The Doctor has called in question the accuracy of my accounts of about 35 authors on the whole. It is not possible for me in to-day's lecture to say all that I have to say with regard to his criticisms and those of other scholars. I shall examine only a few important points among them to-day. But before beginning this work I should like to quote two Sanskrit stanzas in this connection:

ಗಚ್ಛತಃ ಸ್ಖಲನಂ ಕ್ವಾಪಿ ಭವತ್ಯೇವ ಪ್ರಮಾದತಃ |
ಹಸಂತಿ ದುರ್ಜನಾಸ್ತತ್ರ ಸಮಾದಧತಿ ಸಜ್ಜನಾಃ ||
ದೋಷಾನುತ್ಸೃಜ್ಯ ದೋಷಜ್ಞಾಸ್ತೃಪ್ಯಂತಿ ಗುಣಲೇಶತಃ |
ಹಂಸಾ ಇವಾಂಬುಪಯಸೋರ್ವೈಲಕ್ಷ್ಯೇ ದುಗ್ಧಪಾಯಿನಃ ||

From this it is not to be understood that I want my mistakes to be overlooked or ignored. What I mean is that sympathy must form a factor in offering criticism if it is intended that it should bear fruit. But in the case of the Doctor I regret to say that it is accompanied very often with ridicule and derision without any cause whatsoever. I shall now begin to answer briefly some of the more important of the criticisms:

1. Nāgachandra, pp. 33-56.
2. Karṇapārya, pp. 71-86.
3. Rudrabhaṭṭa, pp. 94-115.
4. Sumanōbāṇa, pp. 124-49.

Nāgachandra

The period assigned to Nāgachandra by the Doctor, namely, the close of the 10th or the beginning of the 11th century, is evidently due to a misconception. He thinks that Durgasimha, whom he assigns to the period 1024-42, has praised Nāgachandra. This is not so, the poet praised by Durgasimha being Pampa, who is doubtless the author of *Ādipurāṇa* and not Abhinava-Pampa. Having once made this assumption the Doctor has been at considerable pains to find arguments for supporting it and for demolishing my position that Nāgachandra lived at about 1100. I give below a few facts which strengthen the position taken up by me:

(1) According to the Doctor, Nāgachandra lived before 1024, either at the close of the 10th or the beginning of the 11th century. Nāgachandra, however, praises *Ajitapurāṇa* which Ranna wrote in 993, and the way in which he praises it, namely, as *the jewel of a poem* (*Kṛitiratna*), clearly shows that it could not be the work of a contemporary. For the work to attain to such celebrity some reasonable period, say at least half a

century, has to be postulated. This makes it impossible for Nāgachandra to have lived before 1024. Again, Durgasimha, who lived at about 1024, does not mention Ranna, evidently because he was then too recent a poet to deserve mention. Such being the case, is it conceivable that Nāgachandra, who preceded Durgasimha (c. 1024), would praise Ranna's work in such flattering terms? We are thus led to the conclusion that the assumption of the Doctor is untenable.

(2) There is an important statement made by Karṇapārya, the author of *Nēmināthapurāṇa* (I, 101), about Nāgachandra which affords decisive evidence about his period, namely, that though Nāgachandra was a *modern* (*adyatana*) poet, he was equal to ancient poets. The word *modern* can only mean that Nāgachandra lived very recently, say about a generation *before* Karṇapārya. The period I have assigned to Karṇapārya being c. 1140 (I, 139), the period of Nāgachandra may be taken to be roughly 1100. But according to the Doctor, who assigns 1174 as the date of Karṇapārya (p. 85), the date of Nāgachandra would be about half a century later than that assigned to him by me. Such being the case, is it reasonable to suppose that Karṇapārya would call Nāgachandra who, according to the Doctor, lived before 1024, a *modern* poet?

(3) Nāgachandra praises a Jaina Guru named Mēghachandra-traividya in I, 20 of his *Rāmāyaṇa*, and we learn from Sravaṇa Beḷgoḷa inscription 127, of about 1115, that the same guru died in 1115. There can be no manner of doubt about the identity of the guru, since the verse in which Nāgachandra praises him also occurs in connection with the guru in the inscription. If Nāgachandra had lived before 1024, would it have been possible for him to praise a man who died nearly a century after that period? The Doctor tries to get over the difficulty by making the curious statement that the composers of the inscriptions kept quiet for a full century and then began to use the verses of Nāgachandra in connection with other gurus of the same name (p. 47). This is simply ridiculous and a gratuitous insult to Jaina writers. The

natural inference is that Nāgachandra lived at about 1100. This will easily explain the instance of Śrutakīrti given by the Doctor (p. 45).

(4) An author named Mēghachandra is stated to have written in 1148 an easy Kannaḍa commentary on Pūjyapāda's *Samādhi-śataka* for the use of the son of the celebrated Pampa (*Ind. Ant.*, XII. 20). The reference here is clearly to Nāgachandra and the statement fixes his period as about 1100. This Mēghachandra is most probably identical with the one mentioned in Śravaṇa Belgoḷa 66 as the oldest disciple of Nayakīrti and as a colleague of Adhyātmi-Bālachandra. The doctor's statement that Adhyātmi-Bālachandra lived in 1231 has no basis to stand upon.

(5) Finally, as already stated by me (I, 449), there is every probability of the inscription of Vikramāditya VI (1076–1126), No. A. 23, kept in the Bijapur Museum, having been written by Nāgachandra, judging from the close similarity in idea and expression of several verses of the inscription to those in *Pampa-Rāmāyaṇa* (see p. 36 below.) This fact, too, leads us to the inference that Nāgachandra should have flourished at about 1100.

There are also a few more points dealt with by the Doctor incidentally in his article on Nāgachandra (pp. 36–42 and 52–56), which have now to be briefly noticed. He rightly criticises my identification of some of the Jaina Gurus with others of the same name, such as that of Mēghachandra-traividya of S.B. 127, who died in 1115, with his namesakes mentioned in S.B. 69 and 66, and that of Bālachandra of Vakra-gachchha with Śubhakīrti's father Bālachandra of S.B. 140 (I, 102–3). My chief object in this connection has been to show that there were two Bālachandras, one of Vakra-gachchha who was the guru of Nāgachandra and lived at about 1100, and the other of Pustaka-gachchha who lived at about 1180. The Doctor, however, makes the assumption that these two gurus were contemporaries and tries to adjust facts to this preconceived notion of his. He begins by stating (p. 36) that the date of S.B. 69, given by me as about 1100, must be about 1180. This inscription is not dated. It tells us that Bālachandra of Vakra-gachchha was a colleague of Gauḷadēva, who was a disciple of Gōpanandi, though at the close it likewise says that he was a colleague of Triratnanandi, a disciple of Māghanandi who was a colleague of Gōpanandi. In either case it is clear that Bālachandra of Vakra-gachchha came immediately after Gōpanandi and was not removed from him by a long interval of time. Now, Chennarāyapaṭṇa 148 records a grant to this same Gōpanandi by the Hoysaḷa King Eṟeyanga, son of Vinayāditya, in 1094. Consequently the period of Bālachandra of Vakra-gachchha may safely be taken to be about 1100 which is exactly the date that I have assigned to S.B. 69. And this must also be the approximate period of his disciple Nāgachandra.

The Doctor quotes three inscriptions in support of his assumption that Vakra-gachchha Bālachandra was a contemporary of Adhyātmi Bālachandra who lived in about 1180. But from what has been stated above, it is clear that his assumption is wrong. Let us see what these inscriptions have to say in the matter. The first is an inscription at Kalasāpura, published on pp. 36–39 of the *Mysore Archæological Report* for 1923, which records a grant to a Jaina guru named Bālachandra in 1176 by Kavaḍamayya's Dēviseṭṭi, on behalf of the Vīraballāla-Jinālaya erected by himself. After giving the spiritual pedigree of Vakra-gachchha Bālachandra just like S.B. 69, the inscription proceeds to say that his lay disciple was Kavaḍamayya's Anuvantayya and that four generations after the latter (details partly gone) came Kavaḍamayya's Dēviseṭṭi, the donor. It will thus be seen that Vakra-gachchha Bālachandra, who was the guru of Kavaḍamayya's Anuvantayya, an ancestor of Kavaḍamayya's Dēviseṭṭi, cannot be identical with Bālachandra, the contemporary of the donor. This Bālachandra was evidently Adhyātmi Bālachandra who, as we know from S.B. 234, of about 1180, was a contemporary of Kavaḍamayya's Dēviseṭṭi. The second inscription is Bēlūr 129 of 1196. This records a grant by certain persons for the God Mallinātha set up by them in the enclosure of the

Sāntinātha-basti erected by Kavaḍamayya's Dēvisetṭi. This grant may have been made after Dēvisetṭi's time. The inscription begins with a verse in praise of Vakra-gachchha Bālachandra and states that some land was purchased by the donors from Rāmachandra, disciple of Bālachandra of Mandavi. The Doctor hastily concludes from this that Vakra-gachchha Bālachandra lived at the time of the record, i.e., in 1196 and that he was identical with Bālachandra of Mandavi. Such is not at all the case. The verse in praise of Vakra-gachchha Bālachandra occurs at the beginning because he was, as we saw in the Kalasāpur inscription, the *Kula-guru* of Kavaḍamayya's Dēvisetṭi. I need not say that Bālachandra of Mandavi has nothing to do with his namesake of Vakra-gachchha; nor has he anything to do with Adhyātmi Bālachandra; he appears to be a different man altogether. The third inscription, S.B. 186, registers a grant in 1231 by Gommaṭa-Seṭṭi, son of Paduma Seṭṭi who was a lay disciple of Adhyātmi Bālachandra. It will be seen that this grant was made two generations after Adhyātmi Bālachandra and consequently there is no ground to suppose, as the Doctor has done, that he lived in 1231.

The Doctor takes me to task for using the word *nūta* in the sense, as he thinks, of *Nūtna* and writes two pages (53–54) on the matter for my edification. Any one who had paid some attention to the synonym *abhinava* given by me for *nūta* and to the distinction that I make between *nūta* and *vinūta*, which are but synonyms (I, 100), would at once see that *nūta* was but a printer's mistake for *nūtna*. The Doctor may have had the charity of crediting me with a little knowledge of Sanskrit though not with as high a proficiency in it as his own.

He also asserts (pp. 55–56) that we have to believe that Nāgachandra was himself the author of *Jinamunitanaya* till satisfactory evidence to the contrary is forthcoming. He argues thus: 'Though there is no similarity between the style of Ponna's *Sāntipurāṇa* and that of *Jināksharamāle*, the latter work is believed to be his. Similarly, Nāgachandra's authorship of *Jinamunitanaya* has to be believed though the styles of his other works and this are not similar.' Any Kannaḍa scholar who is sufficiently familiar with classical poems in that language will at once see that there is perfect similarity in the styles of Ponna's two works, whereas the styles of Nāgachandra's other works and *Jinamunitanaya* are as dissimilar as anything can be. He will never do the injustice of attributing such modern forms as *Kēḷuva*, *pēḷuva chinumaya* and *koluvam* to Nāgachandra, besides grammatical errors of various kinds. I am constrained to say that in this matter the Doctor is not competent to pronounce an opinion.

Comparison of a few verses of the Bijāpur inscription with those of Pampa-Rāmāyaṇa.

BIJĀPUR INSCRIPTION, verse 2

ಪಿರಿದಾಯಾಸದಿನಿನ್ನೆಗಂ ತಳೆದ ಧಾತ್ರೀಭಾರಮಂ ವಿಕ್ರಮಾ।
ಭರಣಂಗೊಪ್ಪಿಸಿ ಬೀೞ್ಪುದಂ ಪಡೆದುವೆಂತಾಸುಂ ದಿಶಾದಂತಿ ದಿ॥
ಕ್ಕರಿಣೀಪೀಚಕ ಚುಂಬನೈಕ ಸುಖಮಂ ಶೇಷೋರಗಂ ಭೋಗಿಸೀ।
ಪರಿರಂಭೋತ್ಸವಮಂ ಪುರಾಣಕಮಠಂ ನಿದ್ರಾಂಗನಾಸಂಗಮಂ॥

PAMPA-RĀMĀYAṆA, VI, 84

ಧರೆಯುಂ ದ್ವಾದಶಚಕ್ರವರ್ತಿಗಳಿನಿತ್ತಲ್ ದೇವ ನಿಮ್ಮೀ ಭುಜಾ।
ಪರಿಘಕ್ಕೊಪ್ಪಿಸಿ ಬೀೞ್ಪುದಂ ಪಡೆದುವೆತ್ತಾಸುಂ ದಿಶಾದಂತಿ ದಿ॥
ಕ್ಕರಿಣೀಪೀಚಕ ಚುಂಬನೈಕ ಸುಖಮಂ ಶೇಷೋರಗಂ ಭೋಗಿಸೀ।
ಪರಿರಂಭೋತ್ಸವಮಂ ಪುರಾಣಕಮಠಂ ನಿದ್ರಾಂಗನಾಸಂಗಮಂ॥

BIJĀPUR INSCRIPTION, verse 20

ಆಕ್ಷೋಣೀಧರಪದುವ್ರಂ (?) ದಕ್ಷಿಣದಿಙ್ಮುಖದೊಳೆಸೆವ ಶಶಿಖಂಡದವೊಲ್।
ಲೀಕ್ಷಣಸುಖಮಯಮಿರ್ಪುದು। ದಕ್ಷಿಣಭರತ ತ್ರಿಖಂಡದಾರ್ಯಾಖಂಡಂ॥

PAMPA-RĀMĀYAṆA, I, 45

ಆಕ್ಷೋಣೀಧರವಲ್ಲಭ। ದಕ್ಷಿಣದಿಙ್ಮುಖದೊಳೆಸೆದು ಶಶಿಖಂಡದವೊಲ್।
ಲೀಕ್ಷಣಸುಖಮಯಮಿರ್ಪುದು। ದಕ್ಷಿಣಭರತ ತ್ರಿಖಂಡದಾರ್ಯಾಖಂಡಂ॥

BIJĀPUR INSCRIPTION, verse 1

ಶ್ರೀಮಚ್ಚಳುಕ್ಯವಂಶಲ। ಲಾಮಂ ಚತುರುದಧಿಮೇಖಲಾಲಂಕೃತ ಧಾ।
ತ್ರೀಮಂಡಲಮಂ ವಿಕ್ರಮ। ಧಾಮಂ ನಿಜಭುಜಚಕ್ರಪಾಣದಿಂ ರಕ್ಷಿಸಿದಂ॥

PAMPA-RĀMĀYAṆA, X, 77

ಚತುರುದಧಿಮೇಖಲಾಲಂ | ಕೃತವಸುಧೆಯನಾಳ್ದು ಪಡೆದು ಸುತರಿನ್ನರನಾ |
ಜಿತಶತ್ರು ವಿಜಯಸಾಗರ | ರತರ್ಕ್ಯಭುಜವೀರ್ಯರರಸುಗೆಯ್ಯುತ್ತಿರ್ದರ್ ||

PAMPA-RĀMĀYAṆA, II, 39

ಚತುರುದಧಿಮೇಖಲಾಲಂ | ಕೃತವಸುಧಾ ದೇವಿಗಜ್ಜ ಗಾಪಿಸವರ್ ದಿ |
ಕ್ಷಿತಿಗಳೆನಿಸೆ ಸಾರ್ವಭೌಮರೋ | ಸ್ಥಿತಿಯಂ ತಳೆದಂ ಸುಕೌಶಲಕ್ಷ್ಮಿತಿನಾಥಂ ||

Karṇapārya

As regards Karṇapārya, I may state at once that my identification of some of the gurus mentioned by him with their namesakes in the Śravaṇa Beḷgoḷa inscriptions is not quite correct. My statement that the Śilāhāra King Gaṇḍarāditya had the other names Gōvardhana, Gōpaṇa and Srībhūshaṇa and that he had four sons, namely, Vijayāditya, Lakshmaṇa, Vardhamāna and Śānta must have been made on the authority of some manuscript that I have used, though the two manuscripts A. 52 and 4 of *Nēmināthapurāṇa*, now available in the Mysore Oriental Library, which are identical with each other, do not give this information. I have been trying to procure another manuscript of the work for the last six months, but without success. In the meanwhile, I may mention, however, that the Eksambi inscription of Vijayāditya, of 1165 (*Mysore Archæological Report* for 1916, 48-50), which has been referred to by the Doctor (p. 85), states that Vijayāditya was the eldest son of Gaṇḍarāditya, thus showing that the former had a younger brother or brothers. Further, the title Rūpanārāyaṇa of Gaṇḍarāditya and Vijayāditya was also borne by Lakshmaṇa (p. 80, verse 27), though he did not succeed to the throne. Again, my statement that both Karṇapārya and Nēmichandra were patronised by the Raṭṭa King Lakshmīdēva of Saundatti (I, Kannaḍa Introduction, 17, *Mysore Archæological Report* for 1916, 50) as also the statement that the two poets wrote their works under the patronage of the Śilāhāras (II, English and Kannaḍa Introductions, 10 and 16 respectively) requires correction. Karṇapārya was patronised by Lakshmaṇa or Lakshmīdēva during the rule of the Śilāhāra king

Vijayāditya and Nēmichandra by King Lakshmīdēva, son of the Raṭṭa King of Saundatti, Kārtavīrya III. The cause of the confusion can easily be realised when one thinks of the identity of the names (Lakshmīdēva) of the two chiefs, as also of the identity of the names (Chandrikādēvi) of their wives.

With regard to the period of Karṇapārya, as stated before, he wrote his work during the reign of Vijayāditya. We learn from inscriptions that Vijayāditya ruled in the years 1143, 1153 (*Dynasties of Kanarese Districts*, 545) and 1165 (Eksambi inscription, mentioned above). But as Karṇapārya says that he wrote his work at the instance of Śrībhūshaṇa (Gaṇḍarāditya), it is likely that the composition of his work was begun sometime before 1143. I have therefore given c.1140 as the poet's date. There is no ground for the date 1174, given by the Doctor.

The Doctor thinks that the titles, Paramajinamatakshīravārāśichandra and Bhavyavanajavana-mārtāṇḍa, do not belong to the poet but to his patron, Lakshmaṇa; but I do not think that Kannaḍa scholars who are familiar with the ways of Jaina poets will agree with him.

The period of Karṇapārya mentioned by Durgasimha (c.1025) as the author of *Mālavīmādhava* may be taken to be about 1000.

Rudrabhaṭṭa

With regard to the period of Rudrabhaṭṭa (I, 269), the Doctor has come, step by step, to the conclusion that the poet wrote his work in about 1218–19 (pp. 95–115) and not in about 1180, as stated by me. Briefly his arguments may be stated thus:

(1) The earliest available inscription naming Umādēvi, the Queen of Ballāḷa II, is dated 1185. She could not have been his queen in 1180. So Rudrabhaṭṭa who mentions her must have written his work after 1185 (p. 101).

(2) The attribute, Paramaiśvaryāspadam, applied to Ballāḷa II by the poet in the second of the invocatory verses of his *Jagannāthavijaya*, indicates that the king had the paramount title Paramēśvara when the poet

wrote. Ballāḷa II began to assume paramount titles in 1190 after defeating the Sēvuṇa king Bhillama. Consequently the poet must have written after 1190 (p. 102).

(3) The attribute Rājarājapratishṭhāniratam applied to Ballāḷa II in the second invocatory verse, refers to the establishment of the Chōḷa King Rājarāja III (1216-46) on the throne, which he had lost, during the reign of the King, by his son Narasimha II. This event together with the conquest of the Magara Kingdom must have taken place in 1217 as Nāgamangala 29, of 1218, applies the titles, Chōḷarājyapratishṭhāchārya, Magararājyadiśāpaṭṭa and Pāṇḍyagajakēsari, to Ballāḷa II (p. 113). Ballāḷa II bore these titles in consequence of the conquests made by his son Narasimha II in 1217 (p. 114). Rudrabhaṭṭa, who mentions the establishment of Rājarāja III on the throne, which took place in 1217, must have lived after that date and before the death in 1220 of Ballāḷa II, i.e. in about 1218-19.

Here follow my answers to the Doctor's arguments:

(1) The fact that an inscription of 1185 mentions Umādēvi does not preclude the possibility of her having been the queen of Ballāḷa II some years before the date of that inscription, say, in about 1180. An inscription of an earlier date mentioning queen Umādēvi may turn up at any moment. My date for Rudrabhaṭṭa is not exactly 1180, but *about* 1180, which allows a latitude of a few years on both sides.

(2) I do not believe that Rudrabhaṭṭa intended to convey the sense read into it by the Doctor by the use of the attribute, Paramaiśvaryāspadam, which merely means 'the abode of power or wealth.' If it was intended to mention the distinctive paramount title Paramēśvara, the poet would have used the form Pāramaiśvarya, the state of being Paramēśvara, with a long vowel in the first syllable. Further, paramount titles such as Chakravarti (emperor) are applied to Ballāḷa II even in inscriptions of an earlier date than 1190, e.g., SB. 240, of about 1175; No. 35, *Mysore Archæological Report* for 1926, of 1183, No. 5, same *Report* for 1923, of 1185. There are likewise inscriptions of a later date than 1190 which apply

only the subordinate title Mahāmaṇḍalēśvara to the same king, e.g., Nanjangūd 71 of 1192: S.B. 335, of 1195; Tirumakūḍalu-Narasīpur 31, of 1195–96.

(3) It is not at all likely that, as stated by the Doctor, Rudrabhaṭṭa had in his mind the establishment of the Chōḷa King, Rājarāja III (1216–46), on the throne by Ballāḷa II's son Narasimha II in 1217 when he applied the attribute Rājarājapratishṭhāniratam to Ballala II. The expression simply means 'intent on establishing *great kings* (on their thrones)' and does not refer to any particular historical event. We must remember that when Rudrabhaṭṭa wrote his work Umādēvi was the queen of Ballāḷa II and Chandramauḷi his minister. We can approximately determine from the inscriptions the period of Umādēvi to be 1185–1209. The period of Chandramauḷi, at whose instance *Jagannāthavijaya* was written, as stated by the poet himself, is a very important point in the matter under discussion. From the available inscriptions in which Chandramauḷi is mentioned, namely, S.B. 327 of 1181, Chennarāyapaṭṇa 150, of 1182, and Arsīkere 127, of 1185, we learn that his period was about 1181–85. No inscription of a later date mentioning him has been met with. We may not therefore be far wrong in supposing that Chandramauḷi did not continue as minister of Ballāḷa II much longer than the period noted above, and that the composition of *Jagannāthavijaya* must consequently have taken place about the same period and not in about 1218–19, nearly 35 years after that period.

Further, as far as I know, there is no epigraphical evidence to show that either Ballāḷa II or his son Narasimha II or any of his successors had the title Rājarājapratishṭhānirata, though Narasimha II deserved it by reason of his having placed Rājarāja III on the throne of his ancestors, instead of the general title Chōḷarājyapratishṭhāchārya which is invariably applied to him. Another distinctive title applied to him is Magararājyanirmūlana, by reason of his conquest of that kingdom. These two distinctive titles, together with the title Pāṇḍyagaṇḍaśailavajradaṇḍa or one of similar import in some cases, are correctly applied to Narasimha II in numerous inscriptions such as Chennarāyapaṭṇa 197 and 203, of 1223; Chennagiri 72, of 1221, Dāvaṇgere 25, of 1224: and Gubbi 45, of 1233, though these three titles are by mistake applied to Ballāḷa II in the solitary inscription[1] Nāgamangala 29, of 1218. The Doctor says (p. 114) that Ballāḷa II assumed these titles, namely, Chōlarājyapratishṭhāchārya, Magararājyadiśāpaṭṭa and Pāṇḍyagajakēsari, by reason of the conquests of his son Narasimha II in 1217. The usual practice, however, is for the son to inherit the titles of the father and not vice versa. In another place (p. 110) the Doctor states that the title Pāṇḍyagaṇḍaśailavajradaṇḍa or others of similar import such as Pāṇḍyagajakēsari, Pāṇḍyarājadiśāpaṭṭa and so on, were *for the first time* borne by Ballāḷa II and subsequently assumed by his son and grandson. This statement is wrong, since such titles had been borne by the father and grandfather of Ballāḷa II as evidenced by inscriptions; e.g. Nāgamangala 76 (1145) styles Vishṇuvardhana Pāṇḍyakulapayōdhibaḍabānalam; and Kadūr 96 (1141) Pāṇḍyagaṇḍagarvaparvata-Pākaśāsanam; S.B. 345 (c. 1159) and Kṛishṇarājapēte 53 (1171) apply the title Pāṇḍyakulakamala-vētaṇḍa to Narasimha I. This same title of his father is applied to Ballāḷa II in S.B. 327 (1181) and 335 (1195), Arsīkere 90 and 93, of 1189, Chennarāyapaṭṇa 78 (1185) and so forth.

It will thus be seen that no valid reason has been given for changing the date assigned by me to Rudrabhaṭṭa, namely, c. 1180, though I would myself change it to c. 1185 to bring it into line with the period of Umādēvi and Chandramauḷi.

Sumanōbāṇa

About Sumanōbāṇa the Doctor has written a great deal, 26 pages (124–49), most of which is quite irrelevant to the matter on hand. He has made some guesses based on a misinterpretation of the following verse occurring in Janna's *Anantanāthapurāṇa* (I, 162, 329):

[1] The date of Arsikere 183 is doubtful.

ಜನನಾಥಂ ಜಗದೇಕನಲ್ಲಿ ಕಟಕೋಪಾಧ್ಯಾಯನಾ ನಾಗವ|
ರ್ಮನಿದಾನೀಂತನಶರ್ವವರ್ಮನೆ ಗಡಂ ಜನ್ನಂಗುಪಾಧ್ಯಾಯನಿಂ||
ದು ನೃಸಿಂಹ ಕ್ಷಿತಿಪಾಲನಲ್ಲಿ ಕಟಕೋಪಾಧ್ಯಾಯನಾರೆಂಬ ನೂ|
ಕ್ತಿನವೀನೋಜ್ವಲ ಬಾಣನಪ್ಪ ಸುಮನೋಬಾಣಂ ಕವಿಶ್ರೇಷ್ಠರೊಳ್||

Any Kannaḍa scholar will see at once that the verse consists of two sentences, one ending with Upādhyāyam and the other comprising the remaining portion, and interpret it thus: 'The famous Nāgavarma who was the Kaṭakōpādhyāya (poet-laureate) of King Jagadēkamalla and who was verily the Śarvarvama of modern times was Janna's teacher. Do you ask who at present is the Kaṭakōpādhyāya of King Nṛisimha? (He is) one of the best poets Sumanōbāṇa who is a brilliant modern Bāṇa in speech.' There are two events mentioned here, one a past and the other a present. But the Doctor would divide the verse into two parts, one ending with Nāgavarmam and the other comprising the rest of the verse, and take the verse to mean that Nāgavarma was the Kaṭakōpādhyāya of King Jagadēkamalla, and that Sumanōbāṇa, a Śarvavarma of modern times, the teacher of Janna, a modern Bāṇa, was the Kaṭakōpādhyāya of King Nṛisimha. No person who has any knowledge of Kannaḍa poetry will accept this interpretation. Verse 423 of Nāgavarma's *Kāvyāvalōkana* (I, 145) applies to him the epithet Abhinava Śarvavarma by reason of his approved works on grammar, Śarvavarma being an ancient grammarian who wrote the *Kātantra*. So the epithet Idanīntana-Śarvavarma used by Janna, which is nothing but a synonym of the other epithet, can apply only to Nāgavarma and not to Sumanōbāṇa. Consequently the expression 'Janna's teacher' has also to be taken to apply to Nāgavarma alone. In his *Yaśōdharacharite* Janna says that he was the son of Sumanōbāṇa and in his *Anantanāthapurāṇa* that he was the son of Śankara; we have therefore to identify Sumanōbāṇa with Śankara as we know that both the works were written by one and the same poet. But the Doctor would have the two as different persons and take the word *son* in the expression, 'the son of Sumanōbāṇa,' in the sense of a disciple, to make it accord with his assumption that 'Janna's teacher' in the above verse referred to Sumanōbāṇa. In spite of the Doctor's misinterpretation and assumption to the contrary, Janna was the son of Sumanōbāṇa and closely related to Mallikārjuna and Kēśirāja who were undoubtedly Jainas, as evidenced, among other things, by the invocatory verse in *Sūktisudhārṇava* and the description of sound as a substance of white colour in sutra 9 of *Śabdamaṇidarpaṇa*. The Jainas will never consider Saivas as members of their own community.

With regard to the period of Sumanōbāṇa, I have to state that he was the Kaṭakōpādhyāya, not of Narasimha I (I, 162), but of Narasimha II (1220-35) as indicated by the word *indu* (at present) used by Janna in the above-mentioned verse. He may have lived in the early years of this king's reign, but his period must be taken back to at least 1175, since his son Janna, who composed the inscription Chennarāyapaṭna 179 in 1190, must have been 25 or 30 years old at that time. This shortens the interval of 95 years given by the Doctor between Sumanōbāṇa (c. 1150) and his son-in-law Mallikārjuna (c. 1245) by 25 years, and if we suppose, as we may reasonably do, that 1245 represents the 30th or 40th year after Mallikārjuna's marriage, the interval is further shortened and rendered perfectly normal. Similarly, the query of the Doctor, namely, How can Nāgavarma II (c. 1145) be teacher to Janna of 1230? can be answered thus. A teacher is generally employed to instruct a boy. Will any man in his senses suppose that Nāgavarma II was the teacher of Janna at the time of the composition of *Anantanāthapurāṇa* when he was probably 70 years old? As stated before, Janna must have been 25 or 30 years old in 1190, and there is nothing to preclude the possibility of Nāgavarma II having lived on 25 or 30 years after 1145. We can thus easily establish the contact between the teacher Nāgavarma II and the pupil Janna.

The Doctor then proceeds to say that I am wrong in saying that because Janna was a Jaina, his parents also were Jainas, and gives a few instances of Hindus taking a wife from the Jaina community which have no bearing on the point at issue, since a father's creed is as a rule adopted by the son. He also makes the curious statements that in the period between the 10th and 13th centuries devotees of Śiva and Vishṇu worshipped Jina, and devotees of Jina the deities Śiva and Vishṇu; there was no distinction such as followers of the Vedic path, Jainas and Buddhists; and even though people worshipped Jina or Buddha as the supreme deity, they were still considered to be followers of the Vedic path, and gives in their support a good number of examples (pp. 136–48) from inscriptions of kings and nobles making grants to men and institutions of creeds other than their own, which can only testify to their liberal-mindedness and tolerance, and not to their profession of the other creeds also.

CHAPTER IV

SOME CRITICISMS ANSWERED

(*Continued*)

Nāgavarma

The Doctor has made the assumption, without any solid ground, that only one author of the name of Nāgavarma has written all the five works, namely, *Chhandōmbudhi*, *Kādambari*, *Kāvyāvalōkana*, *Karṇāṭaka-Bhāshābhūshaṇa* and *Vastukōśa*, and that he lived in about 1050. He makes desperate attempts to support this assumption and readily dismisses as wrong or groundless facts that militate against it. His deliberate misinterpretation of the verse *Jananātham Jagadēkanalli* and of the expression, *Bhāḷalōchanam Kavi-Sumanōbāṇana magam* has already been adverted to. The verse clearly says that Nāgavarma was Janna's teacher. If this fact is accepted, the Doctor's theory that Nāgavarma lived in about 1050 has to be given up. So he interprets the verse in his own peculiar way to suit his purpose and makes Sumanōbāṇa Janna's teacher. He further asserts that Jagadēka of the verse refers to Jagadēkamalla I (1015-42). If this be so, it is difficult to make out the object of Janna in mentioning the fact, more than a century old, of Nāgavarma having been the Kaṭakōpādhyāya of Jagadēkamalla I. It is a statement not at all connected with him in any way. In composing the verse Janna's object was to show to the world that he was highly connected, such distinguished personages as Nāgavarma and Sumanōbāṇa being respectively his teacher and father. So the king named in the first portion of the verse cannot be Jagadēkamalla I. Again, in the expression quoted above, which contains the very words of Janna, *magam*, a son, is taken deliberately in the unusual sense of a disciple just to suit his misinterpretation that Sumahōbāṇa was Janna's teacher. It is true that the word 'son' rarely occurs in the sense of disciple in a spiritual succession of gurus, but it can have no such sense here. We now come to a third misinterpretation in the shape of taking a son in the sense of a grandson in the expressions, *Damōdarapriyasutam* and *Damōdaratanayam*. This is done deliberately to support the supposed identity of Dāmamayya's grandson, Nāgavarma, author of *Chhandōmbudhi*, with the author of *Kāvyāvalōkana*, Dāma being taken to be a shortened form of Damōdara. The Doctor seeks support for his queer interpretation in the commentaries on *Dharmaśāstras*, etc. Authors do not write in an enigmatical style to delude their readers. It is rather strange that the author of *Kāvyāvalōkana* names, according to the Doctor, only his grandfather and not his father. It is amusing to read the statement of the Doctor (p. 162) that the reason for the author not naming his father was the necessity for the alliteration in *ma* in the two verses given at foot of the page from *Kāvyāvalokana* and *Vastukōśa*. This is indeed a poor estimate of the capability of the author as a poet. If the poet had really intended a grandson he could, without any detriment to prosody, very easily have expressed the idea by a slight change in the verses such as *Damōdarātmajasutam* and *Damōdarapautram*, without disturbing in the least the alliteration in *ma*.

I have already shown that Nāgachandra lived in about 1100. The author of *Bhāshābhūshaṇa*, who quotes him under *sūtra* 88, must therefore be later than 1100. He also mentions in *sūtra* 73 a Kannaḍa grammarian, Nayasēna, who cannot have anything to do with the Sanskrit grammarian of the same name (pp. 179–81) mentioned in a Mulgunda inscription of 1053 (*Epigraphia Indica*, XVI, 54), but must be identical with the Kannaḍa author, Nayasēna, who wrote *Dharmāmṛita* in 1112. Vikramānka, named in verse 284 of *Kāvyāvalōkana*, must therefore be Vikramāditya VI (1076–1126) and not Vikramāditya IV or Vikramāditya V (pp. 178–9). Further, the author of *Kāvyāvalōkana* quotes two verses, 185 and 547, which name a Nāgavarma who cannot be the author himself, since verses in praise of the author occur only at the end of the chapters and not in illustration of the rules, but must be an earlier author. Again, the author of *Chhandōmbudhi* has the titles Kavirāja-hamsa, Budhābjavanakaḷahamsa, Kandakandarpa and Negaḷtegōja. He is also styled Sayyaḍiyāta. On the other hand, the author of *Kāvyāvalōkana* and *Vastukōśa* has the titles, Abhinava-Śarvavarma, Kavitāguṇōdaya, Kavikarṇapūra, and Kavikaṇṭhabharaṇa. If the authors were the same, as assumed by the Doctor, it is very strange indeed that not one of the former set of titles is found in the latter works, and vice versa. The former author was a great warrior, an Arjuna in battle, while the latter had no such distinction to his credit.

In the last verse of *Kāvyāvalōkana* Chhandōvichiti is named as one of the works of its author, and the Doctor at once concludes that the work is none other than *Chhandōmbudhi* (p. 166). He also advances the amusing argument that because the author of *Kāvyāvalōkana* follows Daṇḍi who has written a *Chhandōvichiti*, he also must have written one (p. 168). He may have written one but it cannot be *Chandōmbudhi* for the reasons given above. If he had written this work, he could have expressed it thus: *Chhandōmbunidhiyalamkriti* instead of *Chandōvichityalamkriti*. The Doctor says (p. 169) that later Chāmuṇḍarāyas were also known as Rāyas. This only shows that they imitated their distinguished predecessor. There is therefore no reason to disbelieve *Bhujabalicharita* which says that the title Rāya was conferred by Rāchamalla on his general for his munificence.

All these facts clearly prove that the Doctor's attempt to support his assumption is a miserable failure, though he would brush them all aside as of no value. In the light of these facts his search for other Rakkasagangas, Chamuṇḍarāyas and Ajitasēnas in support of the supposed period of Nāgavarma, namely, 1050, cannot but prove futile. So, every one of the points urged by me (I. 52-54) for the differentiation of the two Nāgavarmas and their periods stands as strong as ever.

Mallikārjuna

About Mallikārjuna the Doctor says (pp.182-89) that he wrote *Sūktisudhārṇava* in about 1263 and that he was identical with Chidānanda, composer of the inscriptions, Mandya 121 and 122 (I.354). He is wrong in both these statements. The first statement is due to a misunderstanding of the expression, *Elele Mahādēva*, occurring in the verse beginning with *Haṇidam-boyyal* (p.186), which, as any Kannaḍa scholar would understand, does not refer to the Sēvuṇa King Mahādēva (1260-71) but is merely an exclamation of wonder at the prowess of King Sōmēśvara. From Nāgamangala 39 we learn that the defeat of the Sēvuṇa King Mahādēva by Sōmēśvara's son, Narasimha III, took place in about 1271. How can Sōmēśvara who is supposed to have died in 1264 have anything to do with this defeat of Mahādēva? It is true that Sōmēśvara lived for the greater part of his life at Kaṇṇanūr; but he was in the Kannaḍa country in 1236 (*Bombay Archæological Report* for 1897-98), 1237 (*Mandya* 1222) and 1252 (*Mysore Archæological Report* for 1907, p. 4), and might have been there at other periods also. It may perhaps be inferred from the statement of Mallikārjuna that Sōmēśvara, *lord of Dōrasamudra*, approved of his work, in the verse beginning with *Ōrante* (I. 372), that the king heard the work read out to him at Dōrasamudra. Consequently, the date, c. 1245, given by me for the composition of *Sūktisudhārṇava* is not at all affected in any way; it may even be a few years earlier.

The second statement about the identity of Mallikārjuna and Chidānanda, composer of Mandya 121 and 122, is based on a partial similarity of the names and the fact that two of the verses occurring in the inscriptions also occur in *Sūktisudhārṇava*. Mallikārnuja is also known as Malla, Mallapa Chidānanda-Mallikārjuna. In one verse (I. 370) his name occurs in the shortened form; Chidānanda. But the name of the composer of the inscriptions is merely Chidānanda. Mallikārjuna's work being a compilation from various sources, the fact of his having taken two verses from the Mandya inscriptions need not at all raise the presumption that he and the composer were identical. It may be stated here that as Nāgamangala 98, of 1229, contains 16 verses found in Mandya 121 and 122, which are of a later date, the former also may be the composition of Chidānanda, its final portion being illegible. I may also add that verse 810 (I. 355) occurs in Dāvaṇgere 25, of 1224, with the substitution of Narasimha for Sōyidēva, and verse 808 (I. 354) in Kaḍur 12, of 1233, with the substitution of Kali Sōyiballaham for Narasimha-Bhūbhujam. Chidānanda seems to have adapted these two verses from the inscriptions. Again, Mallikārjuna was a Jaina as I have shown before, whereas the composer of the inscriptions was a Brāhmaṇa as indicated by his epithet, *Brahmavidyegāspadarūpam*. The Doctor's surmise that Sumanōbāṇa, Mallikārjuna and Keśirāja may have been Smārta Brāhmaṇas (p. 189) is groundless. I have already shown that they were all Jainas. Otherwise it is difficult to see how the Jaina community could claim them as their own. Sankara, Gange and Janārdana (p. 149) are common enough names among the Jainas. Ranna names a Jaina prince, Sankaragaṇḍa, and says that his own patroness, Attimabbe, excelled him in liberality (I. 66). Gangiseṭṭi and Gangāyi occur in S.B. 235 and 300 as the names of a Jaina man and woman. The names, Sivadēvamma and Janārdana, are even now borne by Jainas. Madhura mentions a Jaina, Mallikārjuna (I. 427), at whose instance he wrote *Dharmanāthapurāṇa*, and Sālva names a Jaina Sankarāmbike (II. 244). The opinion that the names of Keśirāja's works given at the end of his *Grammar* show that he was a worshipper of Siva (pp. 148-49), is rather hasty, as it is not proper to pronounce such an opinion before an examination of those works.

Sōmarāja

My statement that Sōmarāja may have belonged to the Chauta Dynasty (I. 339) is nothing but a mere guess, and I have mentioned it to be so in clear terms. The Doctor asserts (pp. 219–27) that Sōmarāja was a Nuggehaḷḷi chief, and that he wrote his *Udbhaṭakāvya* in 1522 and not in 1222 as I have stated. His chief reasons are (1) that Induśēkhara, a Nuggehaḷḷi chief, mentioned as the son of Rāyaṇa and the grandson of Tirumala of the

Lunar race in Hāssan 117, of 1573, must be the father of our poet, and (2) that *sāsirada nūṟim sanda nālvattu-nālku* (1144) is an alteration made by me, the correct reading according to him being *sāsirada nānūṟ sanda nālvattu-nalku* (1444), which makes the date exactly 300 years later than the date given by me. These reasons are not at all satisfactory. We know quite well from his work that Sōmarāja was a staunch Vīraśaiva. On the other hand, the Nuggehaḷḷi chiefs who are stated in Hāssan 117 to be of the Ātrēya-gōtra, Āpastamba-Sūtra and Yajus-Śākha, cannot be Vīraśaivas, though the names are similar. Further, Hāssan 117 does not name Sōmarāja but mentions Basavarāja as the son of Induśēkhara, and gives his period as 1573. If, as asserted by the Doctor, Sōmarāja was the son of this Induśēkhara, his period, too, ought to be about 1573 and not 1522 as assumed by him. Again, we learn from inscriptions (II. 215) that the Nuggehaḷḷi chief, Rāyaṇa, was a feudatory of the Vijayanagar King Achyuta (1530-42), and if Sōmarāja was this chief's grandson his period would be considerably later than 1522. With regard to the second reason, I may say that I do not at all remember having made any alteration in the verse, though I do not recollect which manuscript I had before me when writing Sōmarāja's life. Even taking for granted for argument's sake that I made an alteration, is not his alteration just to support a preconceived notion more blameable than mine, seeing that I had no theory at all to support? The reading proposed by the Doctor is, however, untenable as it violates grammar. No good author would use the expression, *nūṟ sanda*, instead of the correct form, *nūṟu sanda*. When not compounded with another word, Nūṟu retains its full form as indicated by the exception, *dūṟu puttitu*, given under sutra 82 of the *Śabdānuśāsana*. The same is the case with *Mūṟu*. Compare Pampa—*aṟuvattumūṟu sandandu* (I. 13).

As another ground for his assumption, the Doctor takes (p. 227) Rāyasada Lingarasa, the copyist of *Udbhaṭa-kāvya*, to be identical with Lingamantri (c. 1530), minister of the Nuggehaḷḷi chief, Rāyaṇa, and author of the

Kannaḍa lexicon, *Kabbigarakaipiḍi* (II. 215). Here we have only a partial similarity of names and it is not at all likely that a minister can hold the inferior position of a copyist (Rāyasa). Another point mentioned by the Doctor in support of the theory that Sōmarāja wrote his work in 1522 is that Sālva who quotes Sōmarāja (VIII, 43) in his *Rasaratnākara* lived, according to the Doctor, before 1529 (p. 224), many years before c. 1550, the date assigned to him by me (II. 244). I do not see how this supports the Doctor's theory. From inscriptions, however, we learn that Sālvadeva, patron of Sālva, ruled till 1559 (see *Panchakajjāya*, 162). Consequently the period assigned to Sālva by me cannot be far wrong. The Doctor incidentally states (p. 227), relying on Sāgar 163, of 1488, that Kōṭiśvara (II, 145), who wrote *Jīvandhara-Shaṭpadi* at the instance of the chief Sangama of Sangītapura, lived in about 1480 and not in about 1500 as I have stated. But as this chief, who has nothing to do with Sangirāja of Sagar 163, appears to have ruled after Sālvadeva (Panchakajjāya, 161), his date would be about 1560, and consequently Kōtiśvara's period also has to be brought down to about 1560.

Mr. M. Govinda Pai of Manjēshvar has also published an article on Sōmarāja in *Svadēśābhimāni* (19-8-27 and 26-8-27) and Kannaḍa *Parishatpatrike* (XII, 48-66), stating that the poet wrote his work not in 1222 but in 1522. His main reasons are given thus:

(1) In 1222 the 11th lunar day of the bright fortnight of Āśvija falls on Sunday and not on Wednesday as stated in the verse.[1] But the week-day will be correct in 1522. Therefore the reading must be *nalnūṟ sanda* and not *nūṟim sanda* as I have given. *Nūṟim-sanda nālvattu-nālku* means, according to him, not 100 plus 44 but 100 –44! As I have already stated, the form *nūṟ-sanda* violates grammar. There are numerous instances of inscriptions in which one or two of the constituents given of the date do not fit in, and no scholar thinks it justifiable to bring down the date of the record by hundreds

[1] ವನಜಾರಾತಿತನೂಜವಾಸರದೊಳಾದತ್ತು.

of years just to remedy the supposed defect. In the present case, though the 11th lunar day of the bright fortnight of Āśvīja does not fall on Wednesday in the year Chitrabhānu (1222), it does so in the previous year Vṛisha (1221).[1] Such differences of one year are very common in the dates of inscriptions and literary works.

(2) The interval between Kumārapala or Udbhaṭa (c. 1150), the subject of the story, and Sōmarāja (1222), the teller of the story, is too short for the story to spread from Gujarāt to Karṇāṭaka. I think a period of three quarters of a century is quite ample for the purpose.

(3) The style looks more like that of the 16th century than that of the 13th. This is only a matter of opinion and style cannot be looked upon as a reliable guide for fixing the period of a work in the absence of other evidence.

If, as these scholars have assumed, Sōmarāja wrote his work in 1522, it cannot be explained why he names as his predecessors only poets who lived before 1200 and no one that lived in the three centuries from 1200 to 1500, not even Bhīma (1369), the author of *Basavapurāṇa.* In these circumstances I would prefer to retain the date 1222 for Sōmarāja till irrefutable evidence to the contrary is forthcoming.

Harīśvara, Rāghavānka and Keṟeya-Padmarasa

My conclusion that Harīśvara, Rāghavānka and Keṟeya-Padmarasa flourished at about 1165 (I, 222) is objected to by the Doctor on the following grounds:

(1) Sōmarāja, who praises Harīśvara and Keṟeya-Padmarasa, wrote *Udbhaṭakāvya* in 1522 and not in 1222.

(2) Quotation from Harīśvara's *Girijākalyāṇa* by Mallikārjuna (1263) only proves that the work existed before 1263, and not that Rāghavānka and Keṟeya-Padmarasa lived before that period.

(3) The expression, Narasimha-Ballāḷa of *Padmarāja-Purāṇa,* means 'Narasimha's son Ballāḷa', that is, Nara-

[1] I am obliged to Mr. R. Rama Rao, B.A., of the Archæological Department for this piece of information.

simha III's son, Ballāḷa III (1291–1342), and Biṭṭidēva mentioned there is Ballāḷa IV.

(4) There was a Rudradēva in 1162 whose capital was Anumakoṇḍa and not Ōragallu. There was no Pratāparudra then.

(5) It is not improbable that there ruled, as Brown says, a king named Dēvarāja at Pampāpura from 1286 to 1328 before Harihara I.

(6) As Keṟeya-Padmarasa's father was Basava's contemporary, Keṟeya-Padmarasa, must have been very young in 1165. So he could not have lived during the reign of Narasimha I (1141–73).

(7) It is stated that Harīśvara was sent to Hampe by Narasimha I. But Hampe was not situated in Narasimha I's kingdom, as it was included in the Hoysaḷa kingdom only in Ballāḷa II's time (1173–1220). So Narasimha cannot be Narasimha I.

None of these grounds is satisfactory for the following reasons:

(1) I have already shown that *Udbhaṭakāvya* which praises Harīśvara was written in A.D. 1222 and that Mallikārjuna, who quotes from Harīśvara's *Girijākalyāṇa*, lived in about 1245. So there can be no doubt of Harīśvara having lived before these dates.

(2) I have proved the contemporaneity of Harīśvara, Rāghavānka and Keṟeya-Padmarasa from Vīraśaiva works (I. 222). Rāghavānka was the nephew of Harīśvara; and Harīśvara and Keṟeya-Padmarasa were respectively the accountant and minister of the Hoysaḷa king, Narasimha I.

(3) The interpretation of the expression, Narasimha-Ballāḷa, as meaning Narasimha's son Ballāḷa is not correct. It is only in the Telugu country that the expression conveys such a meaning. Here, however, the word Ballāḷa is used in the sense of Hoysaḷa. In several Kannaḍa works the Hoysaḷas are known as Ballāḷas. So Narasimha Ballāḷa means the Hoysaḷa king, Narasimha (I), and his son Biṭṭidēva means Ballāḷa (II), the grandson of Biṭṭidēva or Vishṇu-vardhana.

(4) In 1162 there was a Kakatīya ruler named

Pratāparudra whose rule extended from 1140-96. This king, according to Telugu scholars, was the author of a Telugu work called *Nītisāra*, and gave an *agrahāra* to Pālkurike Sōmanātha. He is said to have gone to Ōragallu and to have heard the recital of Pālkurike Sōmanātha's *Basavapurāṇa* (Viresalingam Pantulu's *Telugu Poets I*, 217–22). No evidence has been produced by the Doctor for Ōragallu not being the capital at that time. The ruler may have had more than one capital in his territory. The particle *iva* in the verse quoted (*Rajadhānīva*, p. 263) shows that Anumakoṇḍa was only *like* the capital which must therefore have been different.

(5) No epigraphical evidence has come to light in support of Brown's statement that there was a Dēvarāja in Pampāpura, who ruled from 1286-1328.

(6) The contemporaneity of Kereya-Padmarasa's father and Basava does not necessarily lead to the conclusion that Padmarasa was a very young man in 1165, as his father may have been an elder contemporary of Basava.

(7) From the fact that Harīśvara was sent to Hampe by Narasimha I, it does not necessarily follow that that place must be situated within his kingdom. Nor has any evidence been produced for the place not lying within his jurisdiction.

There are a few other points mentioned by the Doctor which also require a word in reply:

He states that because Harīśvara and Rāghavānka do not name Basava, they are not Vīraśaivas. For that matter, Nijagunasivayogi and other recognised Vīraśaivas have not named Basava.

As regards the Doctor's statement that Bijjaḷa was not a Jaina as evidenced by the names, Sōmēśvara and Śankara, borne by his sons, I have already shown that Śankara is a common enough name among the Jainas and the same appears to be the case with the other name also. With regard to the Doctor's query why Mallikārjuna does not quote from Rāghavānka's *Hariśchandrakāvya*, it has to be stated that he does not do so as that work is written in the Shaṭpadi metre, his *Sūktisudhārṇava* consisting of quotations from Champū works only.

The Doctor considers that the statement in *Vīraśaiva* and Jaina works that Basava and Chennabasava were at the court of Bijjaḷa is false, and quotes in support of his assertion Dr. Fleet who has said that Ēkāntada Rāmaiya was probably the founder of the Vīraśaiva faith and not Basava, simply because there was no epigraphical evidence about the existence of Basava. If that be the case, how are we to believe in the existence of Śankarāchārya and Ramānujāchārya who are not mentioned in inscriptions? But fortunately for Basava a new inscription has just been discovered at Arjunavāḍa in the Belgaum Taluk, dated A.D. 1259-60 (Śaka 1182), referring itself to the reign of the Sēvuṇa King Kandhara (1247-60), which mentions Basava, his father, and five generations of his descendants. It thus affords incontestible proof of the existence of Basava at Bijjaḷa's time. The epigraph is published in *Sivānubhava* III, 94.

I do not think any scholar will indulge, as the Doctor does, in such a wholesale condemnation of all Vīraśaiva, Jaina and Brāhmaṇa traditional works and refuse to derive any sort of help from them. Because there are some defects in a work, it is not wisdom to condemn it wholly. Even works which are professedly historical contain such defects. The Doctor is pleased to attribute credulity to me because I quote from Vīraśaiva and other works. Quotation from a work does not necessarily mean a belief in all that is said in it. When the date of a work is known, to say that the authors mentioned in it must have lived before that date is, I think, quite reasonable. Inconsistencies such as those pointed out by the Doctor in Vīraśaiva works are found even in genuine inscriptions.

It will thus be seen that the dates assigned by me to Harīśvaṛa, Rāghavānka and Keṟeya-Padmarasa do not require any alteration.

Other Criticisms

Singirāja

Messrs. Hardekar Manjappa and Sindagi Siddappa, authors of *Srībasavacharitre* and *Srībasavēśvara-charitre* respectively, are of opinion that *Singirāja-purāṇa* is the earliest Kannaḍa account of Basava, Singirāja, the author of this work, being, according to them, identical with his namesake included in the *Dāsagaṇa* (see I. 214 and 294) and thus a contemporary of Basava. In expressing this opinion both of them have relied on a story given by Mr. Basavalinga Śāstri of Mysore in the introduction to his *Singirājapurāṇa-vijaya*, a prose version of *Singirāja-purāṇa*, to the effect that Singirāja, who was a Vaishṇava feudatory of Bijjaḷa, became a convert to Vīraśaivism and wrote *Singirājapurāṇa* and that he was subsequently included in the Dāsagaṇa by Pālkurike Sōmanātha in his *Sahasragaṇanāma*. Mr. Basavalinga Śāstri has not, however, given his authority for the story. As far as I know, there does not appear to be any evidence, literary or inscriptional, in support of the story. Mr. Hardekar Manjappa says in the introduction (p. 6) to his work that I have assigned Singirāja to 1650 in my *Kavicharite*. This statement is not correct: I have assigned this author to about 1500 (Vol. II, 148). It is the generally accepted opinion among the Vīraśaivas that Bhīmakavi's *Basava-purāṇa* is the earliest Kannaḍa work on Basava, and if *Singirāja-purāṇa* had been written before his time, it cannot be explained why Bhīmakavi does not name its author and base his own work on Singirāja's instead of basing it on the Telugu *Basavapurāṇa* of Pālkurike Sōmanātha. No Vīraśaiva authors of an earlier period than the middle of the 16th century name Singirāja, though they invariably name Pālkurike Sōmanātha or Bhīmakavi. The earliest writer who mentions his name is Chennabasavānka (c. 1550), author of *Mahādēviyakkana-purāṇa*. Further, Singirāja criticises some statements relating to Basava, thus showing that there were in existence some accounts of Basava before his time. He would not have done this if he had been the very first writer on the subject.[1] I therefore think that this author cannot be identical with his namesake of the Dāsagaṇa but must be a later writer

[1] When speaking of him, Virūpāksha Paṇḍita (1584) does not say that he was a poet but says merely that he was a great devotee of Śiva (*Chennabasava-purāṇa*, Kāṇḍa 5, Sandhi 2, 50).

of about 1500. Singidēvaiya, another person included in the Dāsagaṇa, has, however, written *vachanas* (p. 352), just like other contemporaries of Basava.

Ratnākaravarṇi

Messrs. Ugrāṇ Mangēśa Rao and Nyāyatīrtha Śāntirāja Śāstri, the editors of *Bharatēśvara-charite* and *Śatakatrayī* respectively, have, relying on Dēvachandra's statement, stated that Ratnākaravarṇi was the author of *Ratnākarādhīśvara śataka*, *Aparājitēśvara-śataka* and *Trilōka-śataka*. Though this belief is common, I have advanced some objections against it and expressed the opinion that Śṛingārakavi-Hamsarāja, the author of *Ratnākarādhīśvara-śataka*, was different from Ratnākaravarṇi, the author of the remaining two śatakas and *Bharatēśvara-charite*, for the following reasons: namely, (1) that the praise of Aparājitēśvara and Mandārasvāmi and the use of the epithets, Niranjanasiddha and Chidambarapurusha, found in what I consider as Ratnākaravarṇi's works, are not found in Hamsarāja's work; and (2) that the guru of Ratnākaravarṇi was Chārukīrti, whereas the guru of Hamsarāja was Dēvēndrakīrti (Vol. II, 274). These objections have not been satisfactorily answered by the above-mentioned editors. In order to identify the two authors, the mention of Mahēndrakīrti as the guru of Ratnākaravarṇi by Dēvachandra has been taken hold of as a point in their favour and they have stated that Mahēndrakīrti and Dēvēndrakīrti, being synonymous, refer to one and the same person. But this view is not at all tenable, since the names are found to refer to different individuals in inscriptions and literary works. Further, the editors assert without quoting any authority that Ratnākaravarṇi had the title Śṛingārakavi-Hamsarāja. Śṛingārakavi does occur as a title and it has been borne by a few poets, but the addition of Hamsarāja to it conveys no sense. So Hamsarāja has to be taken to be the name of a different poet.

Mr. Śāntirāja Śāstri has caused to be printed the colophon which is found at the end of *Ratnākarādhīśvara-*

śataka at the end of the other two Śatakas also, for which there does not appear to be any warrant in the manuscripts I have seen. There is further the clear statement in the last verse of *Trilōka-śataka* that the work was composed by Ratnākarārya. As the expressions Niranjanasiddha and Chidambarapurusha are used as epithets of his *guru* by Ratnākaravarṇi (*Bharatēśvara-charite*, I. 4), my statement that Niranjanasiddha was a title of the author (Vol. II, 274) is not correct. After all the only authority for supposing that Ratnākaravarṇi was the author of all the three Śatakas and that he had the title Sṛingārakavi is Dēvachandra. But this authority is not quite reliable as his work abounds in mistakes. As an instance I may give a statement of his in connection with Ratnākaravarṇi himself, namely, that he was a contemporary of Vijayaṇṇa, the author of *Dvādaśānuprēkshe* (Vol. II, 276). But this is untenable—Vijayaṇṇa's time being 1448 and Ratnākaravarṇi's 1557.

Lakshmīśa

There has been a long controversy in Kannaḍa journals and newspapers about the place, creed and time of Lakshmīśa, the author of *Jaimini-Bhārata*. The generally accepted opinion about the place is that he belonged to Dēvanūr of the Kaḍūr Taluk, which he styles Surapura, Gīrvāṇapura, etc., in his work. He has also dedicated his work to the deity Lakshmīramaṇa of the village. In the temple of this deity, it is said that first honours are shown to him and that portions of his work are recited on certain special occasions as a mark of respect to his memory. His house is even now pointed out in the village. There were until a few years ago his lineal descendants living in the place. In spite of all these facts some have boldly asserted that Surapura in Hyderabad was the place of the author. With regard to his creed, it has been stated that he was either an Advaiti or a Smārta of the Bhāgavata Sect, and not a Srīvaishṇava. As stated before, there were his lineal descendants living in Dēvanūr who were Srīvaishṇavas and no Srīvaishṇava would accept a Smārta for his ancestor. The objection advanced against the author being a Srīvaishṇava is that he praises Śiva, Pārvati and Gaṇapati at the beginning of his work. Instances may be given of other authors, undoubtedly Śrīvaishṇava, who have done the same thing: (1) Lakshma Kavi, the author of *Bhārata*, etc. (p. 15) was a Srīvaishṇava of Hārugadde, Ānekal Taluk, whose descendants are even now *archakas* of the Chenna-kēshava Temple at the village. There can be no doubt of his having been a Srīvaishṇava, as he states that he is a disciple of a descendant of Embār, who was a disciple of Ramānuja; and yet he praises Śiva and Gaṇapati in his work. (2) Timmāmātya, the author of *Ānanda Rāmāyaṇa* (p. 74), was a Srīvaishṇava, whose descendants are even now conducting the duties of *archakas* at Agara, about six miles to the east of Bangalore, and he, too, praises Śiva and Gaṇapati.

Some have observed that Dēvanūr not being an exact equivalent of Surapura, some other place has to be looked for, and their search has led them to Surapura in Hyderabad. These will, however, be surprised when they learn that Timmāmātya has Sanskritised Sādanahaḷḷi into Sahadēvapura, and Lakshma Kavi, Hārugadde into Khagapura. Compared with these renderings the rendering of Dēvanūr into Surapura may be looked upon as the nearest and most appropriate.

With regard to the period of Lakshmīśa, various opinions have been expressed, the balance of opinion being in favour of the date 1415. I have, however, expressed the opinion that Lakshmīśa lived about the close of the 17th century (II. 523). If he had lived in 1415, it cannot be explained why his name is not mentioned by any writer from the 15th to the close of the 17th century: not even by the Brāhmaṇa authors of *Bhārata Rāmāyaṇa* and *Bhāgavata*, and by Chikkupādhyāya, a fellow Srīvaishṇava, who mentions even the Smārta poet Rudrabhaṭṭa. The authors that mention him belong to the 18th century. It is these facts that led me to assign him to the close of the 17th century, which is likewise the period assigned to him by tradition.

Some scholars have made much of the similarities

between his work and the *Chennabasavapurāṇa* of Virūpāksha Paṇḍita (1584) and have concluded that Lakshmīśa preceded Virūpāksha Paṇḍita. But these similarities may be interpreted in either way and do not constitute a decisive factor in determining Lakshmīśa's period.

I may incidentally mention an interesting fact in Kannaḍa literature in connection with a statement made in the Kannaḍa *Parishatpatrike* (V. 5), with reference to Lakshmīśa, that no one would translate a work which was opposed to his faith. I shall give instances of Jainas having written works for their Hindu friends as if they were Hindus and vice versa. Padmarasa, a Jaina (II. 314), wrote, apparently for a Hindu friend, the *Sṛingārakathe* in 1599. At the beginning of the work he praises Sadāśiva, Sarasvati and Gaṇēśa, as if he were a Hindu. Conversely, Pattābhirāma, a Hindu (III. 25) wrote for a Jaina friend, named Paduma, a Jaina work styled *Ratnaśēkharacharite*, in about 1725. The work related a story about the observance of the Pushpānjali vow and the author begins the work with praise of Jina, the Siddhas, etc., as if he were a Jaina.

CHAPTER V

EXTENT AND RANGE OF KANNAḌA LITERATURE

KANNAḌA literature is of vast extent and range. It is a well-known fact that the three classes of poets in Kannaḍa, namely, the Jainas, the Vīraśaivas and the Brāhmaṇas, have, like the authors of the other sister languages of Southern India, written mostly on religion and philosophy. But there are also works, though comparatively small in number, on secular subjects. The Jainas have mostly written accounts of the *Tīrthankaras* and of princes and personages such as Nāgakumāra, Jīvandhara, Sukumāra, Dhanyakumāra, Jāyanṛipa, Jnānachandra, and so on, who attained Ārhantya or Arhathood. In Vīraśaiva works are to be found mostly accounts of the 63 devotees of Śiva and other Śaiva devotees, accounts of the 25 sports of Śiva and expositions of the *Shaṭsthala* and *Ēkōttaraśatasthala*. The Brāhmaṇa works mostly treat of the stories of the the *Rāmāyaṇa*, the *Mahābhārata*, the *Bhāgavata* and other purāṇas, and subjects bearing on the Vēdanta. Bhattākaḷanka (1604) in the introduction to his *Śabdānuśāsana* remarks that in Kannaḍa are written numerous works on *sabdāgama* (grammar), *yuktyāgama* (logic) and *paramāgama* (philosophy) as well as numberless books of poetry, the drama, rhetoric and the fine arts.[1] A survey of Kannaḍa secular literature brings to view not only *kāvyas*, works on poetics, prosody and grammar, and lexicons, but also works bearing on biography and local history, and a respectable number of works on medicine, veterinary science, mathematics and other

[1] ಶಬ್ದಾಗಮ ಯುಕ್ತ್ಯಾಗಮ ಪರಮಾಗಮ ವಿಷಯಾಣಾಂ ತಥಾ ಕಾವ್ಯನಾಟಕಾಲಂಕಾರ ಕಲಾಶಾಸ್ತ್ರ ವಿಷಯಾಣಾಂ ಚ ಬಹೂನಾಂ ಗ್ರಂಥಾನಾಮಪಿ ಭಾಷಾಕೃತಾನಾಮುಪಲಭ್ಯಮಾನತ್ವಾತ್.

sciences and arts. Besides, there are innumerable Kannaḍa inscriptions written in excellent *Kāvya* style. A few details will now be given of the secular works mentioned above in general terms.

The Drama

Bhattākaḷanka says that there were dramas in Kannaḍa during his time. But no old dramas have come down to us. The *Mālavī-Mādhava*, said to have been written by Karṇapārya, and the *Subhadrāharaṇa* and *Prabōdha-chandra*, stated by Kēśiraja as his works, look like dramas. The only drama now extant is the *Mitravindā-gōvinda* of Singarārya (c. 1680), which is a Kannaḍa version of the *Ratnāvali* of Srīharsha. In Telugu *Krīdābhirāmavīdhi-nataka* by Vinukonda Vallabharāya of the 15th century appears to be the earliest drama. In Tamil the early dramas are said to have been lost; and Aruṇāchalakavi of the 18th century, author of *Rāmanātakam*, is looked upon as the father of modern dramatic literature in that language.

Poetics

Among works on poetics the earliest is the *Kavirāja-mārga*. Among subsequent works Nāgavarma's *Kāvyāva-lōkana* treats of verbal ornaments and the ornaments of sense as also of poetical conventions; the *Sṛingāraratnā-kara* of Kavi Kāma, the *Rasaratnākara* of Sālva and the *Navarasālankāra* of Timma, treat of *rasa* or poetical sentiment or flavour; and the *Sāradāvilāsa* of Sālva treats of *dhvani* or suggested meaning. Besides, we have *Mādhavālankāra*, a translation of Daṇḍi's *Kāvyādarśa*, *Apratimavīra-charita* and *Narapativijaya* based on the *Chandrālōka*, a Kannaḍa version of the *Kuvalayānanda*, and other works.

Prosody

The earliest Kannaḍa work on this subject is *Guṇa-gānkiyam*, which has not, however, come down to us. Nāgavarma's *Chhandōmbudhi* treats pretty fully of the subject. There are likewise *Kavijihvābandhana*, *Chhan-*

dassāra and *Nandi-chhandassu* and other works dealing with prosody.

Grammar

There is reference to a grammar written by Nayasēna, but this has not come down to us. Of the works extant dealing with the subject are *Śabdasmṛiti* and *Śabdamaṇidarpaṇa* written in Kannaḍa, and *Bhāshābhūshaṇa* and *Śabdānuśāsana* written in Sanskrit.

Lexicons

The earliest of these is one attributed to Ranna and named *Rannakanda*. *Śabdasāra*, *Karṇāṭaka-Nighanṭu*, *Chaturāsya-Nighanṭu*, *Karṇāṭaka-Śabdamanjari*, *Kabbigara-Kaipiḍi*, *Kavi-Kanṭhahāra*, *Karṇāṭaka-Sanjīvana* and others explain the meaning of Halagannaḍa words; while *Vastukōśa*, *Mangābhidhāna*, *Nānārtha-Ratnākara* and other works give Kannaḍa synonyms for Sanskrit words. Besides, there are commentaries on the Sanskrit lexicons of Amara, Halāyudha, etc., and on lexicons bearing on medicine.

Medicine

The earliest work on medicine is the *Karṇāṭaka-Kalyāṇakāraka* of Jagaddala-Sōmanātha. *Khagēndramaṇidarpaṇa* treats of toxicology. There are also medical works written by Śrīdharadēva, Sālva, Chikkupādhyāya, Vīrarāja, Nanjarāja, Nṛisimhabhaṭṭa, Brahma and others. There are likewise works on surgery and treatment of women and children. Chandrarāja, Abhinavachandra, Rāmachandra and Padmaṇapaṇḍita have written works on the treatment of horses; Kīrtivarma, a Chāḷukya prince, on the treatment of cattle; and Vīrabhadrarāja, a commentary on Pālakāpya's treatment of elephants.

Cookery

The earliest work bearing on this subject is the one written by Jayabandhunandana. Mangarasa and others have also written on the subject.

Astrology, Meteorology

The earliest work on astrology is the *Jātakatilaka* of Śrīdharāchārya. Other works bearing on it and allied subjects are *Lōkōpakāra*, *Raṭṭamata*, *Raṭṭana-Jātaka*, *Narapingaḷi*, *Mārkandēya-purāṇa*, *Śakunaprapancha*, etc. There are likewise commentaries on *Sūryasiddhānta* and other Sanskrit works on Astronomy.

Mathematics

Under this head there are works treating of Arithmetic, Algebra and Geometry written by Rājāditya, Bhāskara, Timmarasa, Bālavaidyada-Cheluva, and others. There are also commentaries on Mahāvīrāchārya's *Gaṇitasārasangraha*, and other mathematical works. Mahāvīrāchārya's work was translated into Telugu by Pāvalūri Mallaṇṇa in about 1200.

Erotics

Under this head the earliest work is the *Madanatilaka* of Chandrarāja. Other works bearing on the subject are *Smaratantra*, *Manmathavijaya*, *Janavaśya*, *Angajabōdhe*, etc. There are likewise commentaries on the Sanskrit works of Vātsyāyana, Kakkoka and others.

Besides the works noted above, there are also treatises on precious stones, palmistry, fireworks, etc.

History, Biography

Among the works dealing with history may be mentioned *Maisūrurājara-charitre*, *Maisūrarasugaḷa-pūrvābhyudaya*, *Chikkadēvarājavamśāvaḷi*, *Keḷadinṛipa-vijaya*, *Biḷigiyarasara-vamśāvaḷi*, *Rājavamśaratnaprabha*, etc., and among those treating of biography may be named *Rājanṛipa-vijaya*, *Kanṭhīravanarasarāja-vijaya*, *Dēvarājēndra-sāngatya*, *Chikkadēvarāja-vijaya*, *Bijjaḷa-rāya-charite*, *Beṭṭavardhana-charite*, *Jagadēvarāyana-kāvya* and so on.

Nāgavarma II's services to the Kannaḍa Language

Before going to the next section, I would say here a word about Nāgavarma II's services to the Kannaḍa language. There are many authors in Kannaḍa who have written excellent poems and several authors who have written on the grammar, poetics, prosody or vocabulary of the language. But it must be said to the credit of Nāgavarma II that he made it his duty to write almost all his works on the language—on its grammar, poetics, prosody and vocabulary—thus proving not only his love for the language but also his solicitude for its propagation. In the whole field of Kannaḍa literature he stands alone in this respect. His works are standard authorities and their importance for the study of the language is acknowledged by all Kannaḍa scholars. His valuable services to the Kannaḍa language are indicated in the following verse, probably composed by an admirer, which occurs at the end of his *Karṇāṭaka-Bhāshābhūshaṇa*:

ಜೀಯಾದಸೌ ಮಹಾಪ್ರೀತ್ಯಾ ನಾಗವರ್ಮಬುಧೋತ್ತಮಃ।
ಯತ್ಕೃಪಯಾಲಂ ಜಗತ್ಯುಚ್ಚೈರ್ಯಾತಿ ಕರ್ಣಾಟಲಕ್ಷಣಂ॥

Jaina Authors in Mysore and in the Tamil and Telugu Countries

Jaina Authors in Mysore

There is pretty good evidence to show that a Jaina colony was established at Śravaṇa Beḷgoḷa in the 3rd century B.C. So Jaina predominance began earlier and, as we know, continued longer in Mysore than in the Tamil country. Several of the early dynasties of kings in Mysore, such as the Gangas, the Rāshṭrakūṭas, the earlier Hoysaḷas, the Kongāḷvas, the Chengāḷvas, etc., were Jaina. The earliest cultivators of the language were Jainas. The oldest works of any extent and value that have come down to us are all from the pen of the Jainas. The period of Jaina predominance in the literary field may justly be called the Augustan Age of Kannaḍa literature. Jaina authors in Kannaḍa are far more numerous than in Tamil. To name only a few, we have Pampa, Ponna, Ranna, Guṇavarma, Nāgachandra, Nayasēna, Nāgavarma, Aggaḷa, Nēmichandra, Janna, Āṇḍayya, Bandhuvarma, and Madhura, authors whose works are

5

admired as excellent specimens of poetic composition. It is only in Kannaḍa that we have a Rāmāyaṇa, and a Bhārata based on the Jaina tradition, in addition to the same works based on Brāhmanical tradition. Besides *kāvyas* written by Jaina authors we have numerous works by them dealing with subjects such as grammar, rhetoric, prosody, mathematics, astrology, medicine, veterinary science, cookery and so forth. Altogether the number of Jaina authors in Kannaḍa is nearly 200. The decline of their political power, which was brought about, among other causes, by the conversion of Vishṇuvardhana to Vaishṇavism, the establishment of the Vīraśaiva faith and the final overthrow of the Kaḷachurya dynasty, produced a check to their literary activity, though works, comparatively inferior, continued to appear in later times.

Jaina Authors in the Tamil Country

We find Jainas in the Tamil country from the Sangam age. Some Tamil scholars are of opinion that the Jainas had immigrated into the southern Tamil districts and made a permanent home there before the first century A.D.; that the golden era of Tamil literature was mostly inspired by the Jainas, as it was also the period when they were in their hey-day of literary and proselytising rigour; that for three centuries down to the 7th century they wielded such enormous influence as to gain the active patronage of the Pāṇḍyan kings for their religion—so much so that many of the Pāṇḍyan kings embraced Jainism and held it up as the state religion; that the influence of the Jainas waned from about the middle of the 8th century on account of the rise of Āgamik Śaivism, and that their final fall in the Tamil districts dates from the 9th and 10th centuries, and was due to the militant preaching of the Vaishṇava Āḻvārs.

Among the Sangam works attributed to Jaina authors may be mentioned *Paḻamoḻi* by Manṟuṟaiyaraiyanar, *Siṟupanjamūlam* by Kariyāśan, *Ēlādi* by Kanimedaviyar and *Nālaḍiyār* by a number of Jaina sages. Iḷangōvaḍigaḷ, author of *Śilappadikāram*, was also a Jaina. According to

Digambaradarśana, a Drāvidasangha was started at Madura in 470 by the Jaina guru Vajranandi, who was a disciple of Pūjyapāda. Three of the five major epics and all the five minor epics are by Jainas. The most admired of the major epics, the *Chintāmaṇi*, is by the Jaina poet Tiruttakkadēvar, whom the Italian missionary Beschi calls the prince of Tamil poets. Further, the grammars *Nēmināthan* and *Nannūl*, the lexicons *Sendan Divākaram* and *Chūḍamaṇi*, and the work on prosody, *Yāpparungalam* and its commentary are all by Jainas. Pavanandi, the author of *Nannūl*, was patronised by Śīyagangan, a feudatory of the Chōḷa King Kulōttunga III (1178-1216). Śīyagangan had the Ganga titles Srīmat-Kuvalālapura-paramēśvaran, Gangakulōdbhavan and Amarābharaṇan, which also occur in inscriptions in connection with the Tamil Gangas of the Kōlār District.

There are some curious stories about the destruction of early Jaina works through sectarian prejudice. There is a tradition that when Śankarāchārya threw Jaina works into the Tunga, one book floated and could not be made to sink. This book was found to be the *Amarakōśa* which was suffered to live on account of its intrinsic merit. There is a similar tradition with regard to *Nālaḍiyār*, a work of the Sangam period. It is said that 8,000 Jaina poets went to the court of a Pāṇḍya king and each wrote a stanza on a scroll. The Hindu poets at the court of the king prejudiced his mind against the newcomers, so much so that the latter decamped leaving their scrolls behind. These scrolls were ordered to be thrown into a river when 400 of them are said to have ascended *for the space of four feet* against the stream. These scrolls were preserved and formed into a work called *Nālaḍiyār*.

Jaina Authors in the Telugu Country

Some Telugu scholars seem to think that there was a Jaina period in Telugu and that almost all the early Jaina works have been lost. The works that are now available are very small in number, not even half a dozen. These are *Jinēndrapurāṇa* by Padmakavi (Prabhāchandra) and *Ādipurāṇa* by Sarvadēvaiya. Atharvaṇāchārya appears to have been a Jaina, judging from his mention of the Jaina authors Hēmachandra, Pūjyapāda and Akalanka. It is said that the work *Kavijanāśraya* bears indications of Jaina authorship.

Patronage of Kannaḍa Literature

From the earliest times Kannaḍa literature, like those of Tamil and Telugu, has prospered under the fostering care of kings and nobles. Among the patrons may be mentioned the Gangas, the Rāshṭrakūṭas, the Western and Eastern Chāḷukyas, the Kākatīyas, the Hoysaḷas, the Raṭṭas of Soundatti, the Silāhāras of Karad, the Kongāḷvas, the Chengāḷvas, the Tuḷuva kings, the Chauṭas, and the kings of Vijayanagara and Mysore; as also the Pāḷegars or chiefs of Ummattūr, Nuggehaḷḷi, Sugaṭūr, Piriapaṭṭaṇa, Madinādu, Bēlūr, Chikkanāyakanahaḷḷi, Mudigere, Bijjāvara, Ikkēri, and Kaḷale. Besides these kings and chiefs, ministers, generals and other officers subordinate to them, and many minor chiefs, have also encouraged literary men. It is also worthy of note that not a few of the above mentioned kings, chiefs and high personages have themselves written works in Kannaḍa and have thus enriched the stock of Kannaḍa literature. These statements will be briefly illustrated by a few examples.

Ādi-Pampa (941) was the court poet of the Chāḷukya chief Arikēsari and was presented by him with the *agrahāra* Dharmapura, situated in Bachche-sāsira. Ponna (c. 950) received the title Ubhayakavi-Chakravarti from the Rāshṭrakūṭa King Kṛishṇa III. Nāgavarma I was presented by Bhōja with horses in appreciation of his poetical skill. Ranna got the title Kavi-Chakravarti from the Chāḷukya King Tailapa (973–97), along with a gold staff, an elephant, a parasol, *chauris*, etc. Brahmaśiva (c. 1100) received the title Kavi-Chakravarti with honours from the Chāḷukya King Trailōkyamalla. Nāgavarma II was the Kaṭakōpādhyāya of the Chāḷukya King Jagadēkamalla II (1138–50).

Rāghavānka was honoured by Pratāparudra I (1140–96) of Wārangal. Pālkurike Sōmanātha received Donkiparti and other villages from the same king. Pārśvapaṇḍita was the court poet of the Raṭṭa King Kārtavīrya IV (1202–20). Sumanōbāṇa was the Kaṭakōpādhyāya of the Hoysaḷa King Narasimha II (1220–35). Madhura was the court poet of the Vijayanagara Kings Harihara II and Dēvaraya I. The latter's minister, Lakshmīdhara, honoured the poet by presenting him with lands, elephants, horses and ornaments. Chāmarasa (c. 1430) was honoured by the Vijayanagara King Dēvaraya II; and Nīlakanṭhāchārya (c. 1485) by the Ummattūr chief Vīrananjēndra. Kavilinga (c. 1490) was the court poet of Sāḷuva Narasinga I. Timmaṇṇakavi (c. 1510) was presented with cloths and ornaments by the Vijayanagara King Kṛishṇadēvarāya. Sālva (c. 1550) was the court poet of the Tuḷuva King Sālvamalla. Rāmachandra, author of *Aśvaśāstra*, and Padmaṇapaṇḍita, author of *Hayasāra-samuchchaya* were patronised by the Mysore King Chāmarāja (1617–37). Tirumalārya, Chikkupādhyāya and the poetesses Honnamma and Sṛingāramma wrote under the patronage of the Mysore King Chikkadēvarāja.

Those who wish to have more detailed information about this matter may refer to pp. 8–15 of the Introduction to Volume II of my *Karṇāṭaka Kavi Charite*.

I may add a few words here about the patronage of Tamil and Telugu Literatures.

Patronage of Tamil Literature

The Chēra, Chōḷa and Pāṇḍya kings, princes, potentates, ministers, military officers and zamindars gave generous patronage to poets and learned men. One or more poets formed part of the personal staff of kings and princes and were given ināms which even their posterity enjoyed in perpetuity. Liberal presents in the shape of money, elephants, palanquins, chariots with horses and flowers of gold were bestowed on deserving poets. Titles of distinction like Āśiriyar (Doctor), Pulavar (Pandit), Kavi-Chakravarti (Emperor of poets), etc., were also conferred upon them. Poets were honoured and respected to such a degree that even kings did not think it dishonourable to act as their palanquin bearers. To appease the wrath of a poet, a Pāṇḍya queen is said to have borne his palanquin one whole night in the disguise of a male carrier. In the Tamil work called *Padiṛ-ṛuppattu*, consisting of ten short poems of the Sangam period, which are in praise of some Chēra kings, mention is made of the rewards got by the poets from the rulers praised by them. To mention a few instances:

The poet Kaṇṇanār of Kumattūr is said to have received from the Chēra King, Imayavaramban Neḍunjēralādan, a grant of the Brahmadāya of 500 villages and a portion of the revenues of the southern districts for 38 years. The poet Kāppiyanar of Kāppiyaru obtained from the Chēra King, Kalangaykkaṇṇi Naṛmuḍichchēral, a gift of 40 lakhs of *pon* and a portion of his kingdom. The poetess Kākkaippāḍiniyār Nachchellaiyar was given by another Chēra monarch, Adukotparttuch-Chēralādan, 9 *kappen*[1] for making jewels and one lakh of gold coins.

Patronage of Telugu Literature

Here, too, the Eastern Chāḷukyas, the Kakatīyas, the Reḍḍis, the Kōmaṭis, the Vijayanagara kings, zamindars, ministers, generals and high officers have patronised Telugu poets and scholars. A few instances are given below. Telugu poets generally dedicated their works to some king or chief. King Rājarāja (1022–63) gave the *agrahāra* Nandamapudi to Nārāyaṇabhatta who helped Nannaiyabhatta in the composition of the *Bhārata*, Pavaturi Mallanna, the translator of Mahavīrāchārya's *Gaṇitasārasangraha*, got the *agrahāra* Navakhandavada. Tikkana Sōmayāji was patronised by Manumasiddhi and Eṛṛapregada was the court poet of Polaya-Vēmareḍḍi. Nachana-Sōma got the village Penchukaladinna from the Vijayanagara King, Bukka I. Srīnātha was the court poet of the Vijayanagara King Dēvaraya II, who bathed him in gold and bestowed upon him the title Kavisārvabhauma. Pillalamarri-Pinaviranna, author of *Jaimini-Bhārata*, was patronised by Sāḷuva-Narasinga I. Allasāni-

[1] Each Rs. 600 weight according to some; 100 *palam* weight according to others.

Peddanna was the court poet of Krishnadēvarāya and had the title Āndhrakavi-Pitāmaha.

Specimens from Kannaḍa Literature

Ādi-Pampa, deservedly called the best of Kannaḍa poets, is thus praised by Nāgarāja (1331) in his *Puṇyāsrava*:

ಪಸರಿಪ ಕನ್ನಡಕ್ಕೊಡೆಯನೋರ್ವನೆ ಸತ್ಕವಿಪಂಪನಾವಗಂ |
ವಸುಧೆಗೆ ಚಕ್ರಿಯಂತಮರಭೂಮಿಗೆ ವಾಸವನಂತೆ ಸಂತತಂ ||
ರಸೆಗುರಗೇಂದ್ರನಂತೆ ಗಗನಕ್ಕೆ ವಿಕರ್ತನನಂತೆ ಧಾತ್ರಿಯೊಳ್ |
ಪೆಸರ್ವಡೆದಿರ್ದನೀಗಳುಮಗೀಗೆ ತದೀಯವಚೋವಿಳಾಸಮುಂ || (I. 32)

The greatness of Nēmichandra and Janna is thus described by Madhura in his *Dharmanāthapurāṇa*:

ಸರ್ವರ ಸಮ್ಮತಮೆನಿಸಗಿದು | ಗರ್ವದ ಮಾತಲ್ಲ ಶಾಸ್ತ್ರಲೌಕಿಕಕಲೆಯೊಳ್ |
ಬೀರ್ವರಿದ ನೇಮಿಜನ್ನಮ | ರಿರ್ವರೆ ಕರ್ಣಾಟಕೃತಿಗೆ ನೀಮಹಾಪುರುಷರ್ || (I. 256)

Chandrarāja and Āchaṇṇa have shown their skill in *Śabda-chitra*, or verbal ornaments, in their works *Madanatilaka* and *Vardhamāna-purāṇa* respectively.

I shall now proceed to quote a stanza each from some of the great poets and a few *Vachanas* from some Vachanakāras:

Guṇavarma I

DESCRIPTION OF THE MOON

ಒಡನೆ ಸುರಾಸುರರ್ ಕನಕಪರ್ವತಮಂ ಕಡೆಗೋಲಮಾಡಿ ಪೋಣ್ |
ಪೆಡೆ ಪಲವಪ್ಪ ವಾಸುಕಿಮಹೋರಗನಂ ಕಡೆಗಣ್ಣಮಾಡಿ ಪಾ ||
ಲ್ಗಡಲನುಪಾಯದಿಂ ಕಡೆಯೆ ರಾಹುಗೆ ವಾಯುಪಥಾಗ್ರಮೆಂಬ ಪೆ |
ರ್ಮಡಕೆಯೊಳಿಕ್ಕಿ ಕೊಟ್ಟ ಪೊಸಬೆಣ್ಣೆವೊಲಿರ್ದುದು ಚಂದ್ರಮಂಡಲಂ ||

(*Kavicharite* I. 25-6)

Pampa I

DESCRIPTION OF THE RAINY SEASON

ಪೊಳೆವಮರೇಂದ್ರಗೋಪದ ಪಸುರ್ತೆಳವುಲ್ಗಳ ತಳ್ತ ಕಾರ್ಮುಗಿ |
ಲ್ಗಳ ಕಿಱುಗೊಂಕುಗೊಂಕಿದ ಪೊಸಲ್ಗಳ ಕೆಂಪು ಪಸುರ್ಪು ಕರ್ಪು ಬೆ ||
ಳ್ಪುಳಕೊಳೆ ಶಕ್ರಕಾರ್ಮುಕವಿಳಾಸಮನೇನೆರ್ದೆಗೊಂಡು ಬೇಟದ |
ತ್ತಳಗಮನುಂಟುಮಾಡಿದುದೊ ಕಾಮನಕಾರ್ಮುಕದಂತೆ ಕಾರ್ಮುಕಂ || (I. 37-8)

Ranna

DESCRIPTION OF THE SPRING

ನವಸಹಕಾರದಂಕುರದಿನಂಕುರಿಸಿತ್ತು ಪೊದಱ್ದು ನೀಳ್ದ ಪ|
ಲ್ಲವ ತತಿಯಿಂದೆ ಪಲ್ಲವಿಸಿತುನ್ಮದ ಭೃಂಗಕುಳಕ್ಕೆ ಕಂಪುವೀ ||
ಱುವ ಕುಸುಮಂಗಳಿಂ ಕುಸುಮಿಸಿತ್ತು ಶುಕವ್ರಜಮುತ್ಸುಕತ್ವದಿಂ|
ಸವಿವ ಫಲಂಗಳಿಂ ಫಲಿತವಾಯ್ತು ಮನೋಜಮನೋರಥದ್ರುಮಂ || (I. 67)

Nāgachandra

DESCRIPTION OF THE BEE

ಬಿರಿಮುಗುಳೊಳ್ ಮುಸುಂಬನಲೆದೊಯ್ಯನೆ ಕರ್ಣಿಕೆಯಂ ಕರ್ದುಂಕಿ ಕೇ|
ಸರಮನೆಱಂಕೆಯಿಂ ಕೆದಱಿ ಬಂಡನುರಂಬರ ಮುಂಡು ತಳ್ತಸಟ್ ||
ಪೊರೆಯೊಳಡಂಗಿ ಸುಣ್ಬರದಿನಾಣತಿಮಾಡಿದುದುನ್ಮದಾಳಿ ತಾ|
ವರೆಯೊಳಗಿರ್ದ ಲಕ್ಷ್ಮಿಯ ಮಸಂಬಡೆದೆಕ್ಕಲಗಾಣನೆಂಬಿನಂ || (I. 110)

Harīśvara

DESCRIPTION OF PĀRVATI ENGAGED IN WORSHIP

ಬರೆದರೊ ಬಯ್ತರೊ ಪೊಲ್ದರೊ| ಪೊರೆದರೊ ಬೆಜ್ಜರೊ ಮರಳ್ಚಿ ಕರುವಿಟ್ಟರೊ ಕಂ|
ಡರಿಸಿದರೊ ಕಡೆದರೋ ಎನೆ| ಗಿರಿರಾಜತನೂಜೆ ಪೂಜೆಯೊಳ್ ರಾಜಿಸುವಳ್ ||
(I. 229)

Rudrabhaṭṭa

DESCRIPTION OF THE CHĀTAKA BIRD

ಮನದನುರಾಗದಿಂ ನೆಗೆದು ನೀಡಿದ ಕಂಠಮರಲ್ದ ತುಪ್ಪುಟು|
ಬರ್ನಿಮಿಷಮಾದ ಕಣ್ ತೆಱೆದ ಚಂಚು ವಿಜೃಂಭಿಪೆಱಂಕೆ ರಂಜಿಸಿ ||
ತ್ತಿನೆ ಸಲವೇಱು ತೋರವನಿ ತಣ್ಪನಿ ಮುಂಬನಿಯೆಂಬ ಕಾರ್ಮುಗಿ|
ಲ್ವನಿಯನಲಂಪಿನಿಂದಮಿದಿರ್ಗೊಂಡು ಕರ್ದುಕಿದುದ್ಘಚಾತಕಂ || (I. 273)

Aggaḷa

DESCRIPTION OF A YOUNG BEE

ಕಿಱುಮಡುಗೊಂಡ ಬಂಡಿನೊಳಗೀಸಿ ಪೊದಱ್ದಿಡಿದಿರ್ದ ಕುತ್ತ್ರಿಸ|
ಱ್ಗಱುವದೊಳೆಯ್ದೆ ಮೆಯ್ಗರೆದು ಕೇಸರದೊಳ್ ಸಲವಿಂ ಪೊರಳ್ದು ಸೀ ||
ಳ್ದಱಗಿದ ಕೀಡಸಟ್ಮಣಿಯೊಳೊಯ್ಯನೆ ಜಾಱು ಪರಾಗ ಪುಂಜದೊಳ್|
ಪಱುವಡಿಸಿತ್ತು ಭೃಂಗಶಿಶು ನೀರಜದೊಳ್ ನಿಜಪಾಂಸುಕೇಳಿಯುಂ || (I. 287)

Dēvakavi

DESCRIPTION OF THE CHAKORA BIRD

ಅರೆಮುಗಿದಕ್ಷಿಗಳ್ ತೆಱೆದ ಚಂಚುಪುಟಂ ನಸುನೋಂಕಿ ನೀಳ್ದ ಕಂ |
ಧರಮಿರದಿರ್ಕೆಲಂಗಳೊಳೆಱಲ್ವ ಪತತ್ರಪುಟಂ ಸಡಿಲ್ದಮೆಯ್ಯ ||
ಸರಲತೆವೆತ್ತು ಪರ್ಚಿದ ನವಿರ್ ಪರಿರಂಜಿಸಲೀಂಟುತಿರ್ದುದು |
ಬ್ಬರಿಸಿದ ಚಂದ್ರಿಕಾರಸಮನಂಚಿತ ಚಾರು ಚಕೋರಸಂಚಯಂ || (I. 318)

Kamalabhava

DESCRIPTION OF CURDS

ಅಧರೀಕೃತ ಶಾರದ ನೀ | ರಧರದ್ಯುತಿಯೆನಿಪ ಕೆನೆಯನೊಳಕೊಂಡಿರ್ಪಾ |
ಮಧುರಾಮ್ಲಮಪ್ಪ ದಧಿಯಂ | ವಿಧುವದನೆಯರೊಸೆದು ನಿಸದಮೆನೆ ಬಡ್ಡಿಸಿದರ್ ||
(I. 365)

Chandrakavi

DESCRIPTION OF MUSIC

ತಿಂಗಳ ಬಿಂಬಮಂ ಹಿಡಿದು ಹಿಂಡೆ ಪಳಿಚ್ಚನೆ ಸೋರ್ವ ಸೋನೆಯಂ |
ತಿಂಗಡಲಿಂ ಪೊದಲ್ದ ಮರ್ದನೆತ್ತಿದೊಡೊಯ್ಯನೆ ಸೋರ್ವ ಸೋನೆಯಂ ||
ಶಂಗಜನಿಕ್ಷುಕಾರ್ಮುಕವನೇಱಿಸೆ ಜುಮ್ಮನೆ ಸೋರ್ವ ಸೋನೆಯಂ |
ತೇಂಗಡ ಸೀಯನುಣ್ಮಿದುದೊ ಗೇಯದ ಪೆಲ್ಲುಲಿ ಜಾಣಗಾಣನಾ || (II. 82)

Mangarasa III

DESCRIPTION OF THE RICE FIELD

ಕಲಮೆಯ ಕದಿರ ಮೀಸಲ ಕಂಪನುಣಲಿಂ | ದಳಿನಿಸುಗಳು ಕೊನೆಯೇಱು |
ಪೊಳೆದುವು ಪೂಗಣೆಯನ ಪಸುಗಾರ್ವಿನ | ತೊಳಪ ನೀಲದ ಮಿಂಟೆಯಂತೆ ||
(II. 182)

Ratnākaravarṇi

DESCRIPTION OF MUSIC

ಒಳಗುಣ್ಮಿದಾನಂದರಸ ತನ್ನ ತನುತುಂಬಿ | ತುಳುಕಿ ಸೋಱಗೆ ಸೂಸುವಂತೆ |
ಕೆಳವನುಱಿಂದ ಬಾಯ್ದೆರೆಯೊಳು ಸುಸ್ವರ | ಸೋಱಿದು ಮೋಹಿಸುತಿರ್ದುದಾಗ ||
(II- 279)

Shaḍaksharadēvc

DESCRIPTION OF THE RICE FIELD

ತೂಗುತೆ ತೊನೆಯುತೆ ಒಳ್ಕುತೆ | ಬಾಗುತೆ ಕಂಪಿಡುತೆ ಕನಕರುಚಿದಾಳುತ್ತುಂ |
ರಾಗಿಸುತೆ ರಂಜಿಸುತೆ ಸೊಂ | ಪಾಗಿರ್ದುವು ಕಣ್ಗೆ ಗಂಧಶಾಲಿವನಂಗಳ್ ||
(II. 445)

Chikkupādhyāya

DESCRIPTION OF THE SUGAR-CANE

ನಳಿನಶರಂ ಸುಧೆಯಿಂ ಪೊಂ| ಗೊಳವಿಗಳೊಳ್ ತೀವಿ ಬೆಳ್ಳಿಯಿಂ ಬಿಗಿದು ಶುಕಂ|
ಗಳ ಕಾಪನಿಟ್ಟವೋಲ್ ಕ| ಣ್ಗೊಳಿಕುಂ ಪುಂಡ್ರೇಕ್ಷುದಂಡತತಿ ಗರ್ದೆಗಳೊಳ್ ||

(II. 478)

VACHANAS

Dēvara-Dāsimayya

ಅಡಗ ತಿಂಬರು ಕಣಕದಡಿಗೆಯಿರಲ್ಕೆ; ಸುರೆಯ ಕುಡಿವರು ಹಾಲಿರಲ್ಕೆ; ಮುಕ್ಕುವರು ಭಂಗಿಯ ಸಕ್ಕರೆಯಿರಲ್ಕೆ; ಸ್ವಸ್ತ್ರೀ ಇದ್ದಂತೆ ಪರಸ್ತ್ರೀಯರಿಗೆ ಅಳಿಪುವರು; ಸತ್ತನಾಯ ಭಕ್ಷಿಸುವ ಹಡಕಿಗರನೇನೆಂಬೆನಯ್ಯ ರಾಮನಾಥಾ.

ಎತ್ತಪ್ಪೆ ಶರಣಂಗೆ; ತೊತ್ತಪ್ಪೆ ಶರಣಂಗೆ; ಭೃತ್ಯನಾಗಿ ಸದ್ಭಕ್ತರ ಮನೆಯ ಬಾಗಿಲ ಕಾದಿರ್ಪ ಸೊಣಗನಪ್ಪೆ; ಕರ್ತಾರ, ನಿನಗೆ ಕರವೆತ್ತಿ ಪೊಡೆವಡುವ ಭಕ್ತರ ಮನೆಯ ಹಿತ್ತಲ ಬೇಲಿಯಾಗಿಪ್ಪೆನೈ ರಾಮನಾಥಾ.

(cp. ತವದಾಸ್ಯಸುಖೈಕ ಸಂಗಿನಾಂ, etc.)

ಹರ ತನ್ನ ಭಕ್ತರ ತಿರಿವಂತೆ ಮಾಡುವ; ಒರೆದು ನೋಡುವ ಸುವರ್ಣದ ಚಿನ್ನದಂತೆ; ಅರೆದುನೋಡುವ ಚಂದನದಂತೆ; ಅರಿದುನೋಡುವ ಕಬ್ಬಿನ ಕೋಲಿನಂತೆ; ಬೆದಱದೆ, ಬೆಚ್ಚದೆ ಇದ್ದಡೆ ಕರವಿಡಿದೆತ್ತಿಕೊಂಬ ನಮ್ಮ ರಾಮನಾಥನು.

Basava

ಹಾವು ತಿಂದವರ ನುಡಿಸಬಹುದು; ಗ್ರಹ ಹೊಡೆದವರ ನುಡಿಸಬಹುದು; ಸಿರಿ ಹೊದ್ದಿದವರ ನುಡಿಸಬಾರದು ನೋಡಯ್ಯಾ. ಬಡತನವೆಂಬ ಮಂತ್ರವಾದಿ ಹೊಗಲೊಡನೆ ತಾವೆ ನುಡಿವರಯ್ಯಾ, ಕೂಡಲ ಸಂಗಮದೇವ.

ವಚನದಲ್ಲಿ ನಾಮಾಮೃತತುಂಬಿ, ನಯನದಲ್ಲಿ ಮೂರುತಿತುಂಬಿ, ಮನದಲ್ಲಿ ನಿಮ್ಮ ನೆನಹುತುಂಬಿ, ಕಿವಿಯಲ್ಲಿ ನಿಮ್ಮ ಕೀರ್ತಿತುಂಬಿ, ಕೂಡಲಸಂಗಮದೇವ, ನಿಮ್ಮ ಚರಣಕಮಲದೊಳು ಸೊಗದ ಬಂಡನುಂಬ ತುಂಬಿಯಾಗಿರ್ಪೆನು.

ವಿಷಯವೆಂಬ ಹಸುರನೆನ್ನ ಮುಂದೆ ತಂದು ಪಸರಿಸದಿರಯ್ಯಾ, ಪಶುವೇನ ಬಲ್ಲುದು ಹಸುರೆಂದೆಳಸುವುದಲ್ಲದೆ? ವಿಷಯರಹಿತನಮಾಡಿ, ಭಕ್ತಿರಸವ ದಣಿಯಮೇಯಿಸಿ, ಸುಬುದ್ಧಿಯೆಂಬ ಉದಕವನೆಱೆದು, ನೋಡಿ ಸಲಹಯ್ಯಾ ಕೂಡಲ ಸಂಗಮದೇವ.

Chikkaiya

ಅಸ್ಥಿ ಚರ್ಮ ಮಾಂಸ ರಕ್ತಪಿಂಡದ ಚೀಲ ಲೆಕ್ಕಕ್ಕೆ ಬರುವುದೆ? ಹುರುಳಿಲ್ಲ ಸಂಸಾರ, ಎಂದಿಂಗೆ ನಾನೀ ಹೊತ್ತ ಹೊದೆಯನಿಳುಹುವೆನಯ್ಯಾ, ಎಂದಿಂಗೆ ನಾನಿದ ಬಳಸಿ ಕಳೆವೆನಯ್ಯಾ, ಎಡಹಿ ಕೊಡನುದಕವ ನಡುನೀರಲ್ಲೊಡೆವಂತೆ ಎನ್ನೊಡಲೊಡೆದು ನಿಮ್ಮನೆಂದಿಂಗೆ ಬೆರಸುವೆನು ಉಳಿಯುಮೇಶ್ವರಾ.

Soḍḍaḷa-Bācharasa

ಗಂಡನುಳ್ಳ ಹೆಂಡಿರ ಕಂಡು ಅಳಿಪದಿರಾ ಮನವೇ! ಬಂದ ಬಸಿಱು ಉಂಡ ಮೊಲೆಯನ್ನು ಕಂಡು ಮಱುಗದಿರಾ ಮನವೇ! ಉದ್ದಂಡತನದಲಿ ನಡೆದ ಭಂಡರನು ಹುಱುಗೊಂಡದಲ್ಲಿಕ್ಕದೆ ಬಿಡುವನೆ ನಮ್ಮ ದೇವರಾಜ ಸೊಡ್ಡಳ.

Urilingadēva

ನಲ್ಲನೊಲ್ಲೆನೆಂದು ಮುನಿದು ನಾನಡಗಲು, ಅಡಗುವೆಡೆಯೆಲ್ಲಾ ತಾನೆ ನೋಡಲಗವ್ವಾ, ನಲ್ಲ ನೀನಿಲ್ಲದೆಡೆಯಿಲ್ಲ; ಅಡಗಲಿಕ್ಕಿಂಬಿಲ್ಲ, ಮುನಿದು ನಾನೇಗುವೆನು? ಶರಣುಗತಿ ಹೊಗುವೆನು ಉರಿಲಿಂಗದೇವನ.

Mahādēviyakka

ಒಮ್ಮೆ ಕಾಮನ ಕಾಲ ಹಿಡಿವೆ; ಮತ್ತೊಮ್ಮೆ ಚಂದ್ರಮಂಗೆ ಸೆರಗೊಡ್ಡಿ ಬೇಡುವೆ; ಸುಡಲಿ ವಿರಹವ, ನಾನಾರಿಗೆ ಧೃತಿಗೆಡುವೆ? ಚೆನ್ನಮಲ್ಲಿಕಾರ್ಜುನದೇವನೆನ್ನನೊಲ್ಲದ ಕಾರಣ ಎಲ್ಲರಿಗೆ ಹಂಗುಗಿತ್ತಿಯಾದೆನವ್ವಾ.

Satyakka

ಇನಿಯಂಗೆ ತವಕವಿಲ್ಲ, ಎನಗೆ ಸೈರಣೆಯಿಲ್ಲ; ಮನವಿಚ್ಛೆಯನರಿವ ಸಖಿಯರಿಲ್ಲ; ಮನ್ಮಥ ವೈರಿಯನು ಭಾವದಲ್ಲಿ ಮನನಿಲುಕಿ ಬಿಡದು, ಇನ್ನೇವೆನಿನ್ನೇವೆ, ದಿನ ವೃಥಾಹೋಯಿತು, ಯವ್ವನ ಬೀಸರ ಪೋಗದನ್ನ ಓಸಾಕಿಯ ತಂದು ನೆರಹವ್ವಾ ಶಂಭುಜಕ್ಕೇಶ್ವರನ.

I shall conclude by giving an amusing extract from Kanakadāsa's *Rāmadhānyacharite*, which is in the form of a dialogue between the grains rāgi and rice regarding their relative superiority; and another comical extract from Mangarasa III's *Samyaktvakaumudi* describing a hearty dinner.

Rice says:

ಕ್ಷಿತಿಯಮರರುಪನಯನದಲಿ ಸು| ವ್ರತ ಸುಭೋಜನಗಳಲಿ ಮಂತ್ರಾ|
ಕ್ಷತೆಗಳಲಿ ಶುಭಶೋಭನದಲಾರತಿಯ ಬೆಳಗುವಲಿ ||
ಕ್ರತುಗಳೆಡೆಯೊಳಗರಮನೆಗಳಲಿ| ಪ್ರತಿ ದಿನವು ರಂಜಿಸುತ ದೇವರ|
ಗತಿಶಯದ ನೈವೇದ್ಯವಾಗಿಹೆನೆಂದನಾ ವ್ರೀಹಿಗ ||
ಜನಪರಿಗೆ ಶಿಶುಗಳಿಗೆ ಬಾಂಧವ| ಜನರೆಡೆಗೆ ಬ್ರಾಹ್ಮರ ಸಮಾರಾ|
ಧನೆಗೆ ವಿದ್ಯಾರಂಭ ಕಲಿಸುವ ಸಕಲ ಭೂಸುರರ ||

ಮನೆಗಳಲಿ ಹರಿದಿನಸದಾಪಾ| ವನಗಳಲಿ ತಾಯೋಗ್ಯನಹುದೆಂ|
ದೆನಿಸಿಕೊಂಬೆನು ನೀನಯೋಗ್ಯನು ಭ್ರಷ್ಟ ತೊಲಗೆಂದ ||
ಹೊಸಮನೆಯ ಪುಣ್ಯಾರ್ಚನೆಗೆ. | . . . ಹಸುಮಕ್ಕಳಿಗೆ ಸೇಸೆಗೆ|
ವಸುಮತೀಶರ ಗರುಡಿಯಲಿ ಶಸ್ತ್ರಾಸ್ತ್ರದರ್ಚನೆಗೆ ||
ಎಸೆವ ವಿಪ್ರರ ಫಾಲದಲಿ ರಂ| ಜಿಸುತ ಗಂಧಾಕ್ಷತೆಯಹೆನು ಭಾ|
ವಿಸಲು ಲೋಕದೊಳಾರು ಸರಿ ತನಗೆಂದನಾ ವ್ರೀಹಿಗ ||

Rāgi replies:

ಸತ್ವಹೀನರ ಬಡವರನು ಕ| ಣ್ಣೆತ್ತಿ ನೋಡೆ ಧನಾಢ್ಯರನು ಬೆಂ|
ಬತ್ತಿ ನಡೆವೆಯುಪೇಕ್ಷೆ ನಿನ್ನದು ಕೇಳಿನೀನದನು ||
ಹೆತ್ತ ಬಾಣತಿಯರಿಗೆ ರೋಗಿಗೆ| ಪಥ್ಯವಾನದಿ ಹೆಣದ ಬಾಯಿಗೆ|
ತುತ್ತು ನೀನಹೆ ನಿನ್ನ ಜನ್ಮ ನಿರರ್ಥಕರವೆಂದ ||
ಮಡದೆಗೆದು ಬೆಳೆಯಡಗಿ ಕ್ಷಾಮದ| ವಿಳಯಕಾಲದೊಳನ್ನವಿಲ್ಲದೆ|
ಯುಳಿವ ಪ್ರಾಣಿಗಳಾದರಿಸಿ ಸಲಹುವೆನು ಜಗವಱಿಯೆ ||
ಎಲವೊ ನೀನೆಲ್ಲಿಹೆಯೊ ನಿನ್ನಯ| ಬಳಗವದು ನಾನೆಲ್ಲಿಹುದೊ ಈ|
ಹಲವು ಧಾನ್ಯಗಳೆನಗೆ ಸರಿಯಲ್ಲೆಂದ ನರೆದಲೆಗ ||
ಸತ್ತವರ ಪ್ರತಿಬಿಂಬರೂಪನು| ವಿಸ್ತರಿಸಿ ಪಿತೃನಾಮಗಳ ನಿನ|
ಗಿತ್ತು ಮೂವರ ಪೆಸರಿನಲಿ ಕರೆಕರೆದು ದರ್ಭೆಯಲಿ ||
ನೆತ್ತಿ ನೆತ್ತಿಯ ಬಡಿದು ಕಡೆಯಲಿ| ತುತ್ತನಿಡುವರು ಶಿಶುಗಳಿಗೆ ನೀ|
ನೆತ್ತಿದೆಯಲಾ ತನುವ ಸುಡಬೇಕೆಂದ ನರೆದಲೆಗ || (II. 240-241)

Description of Dinner

ದೊನ್ನೆಯಂ ಹರಹಿ ಬಾಳೆಲೆ ಹಾಳೆಯಂ ಹಾಕಿ|
ಬಿನ್ನಣದೆ ಮಾಡಿದಾ ಚೌಕದೆಡೆಗಳ ಮುಂದೆ|
ಜನ್ನಿವಾರವ ಮೇಲಕೆತ್ತಿ ಕಿಱುಸುತ್ತುಮಂ ತೆಗೆದು ಸಡಿಲಿಸಿ ಧೋತ್ರಮಂ ||
ಚೆನ್ನಾಗಿ ಯಾಪೋಶನಮನೆತ್ತಿ ಕುಳ್ಳಿರ್ದು|
ಭಿನ್ನರುಚಿಮಾಡಿ ಹರಿಸದೆ ಗಡ್ಡ ಮೀಸೆಗಳು|
ಮಂ ನೀವಿಕೊಳ್ಳುತ್ತೆ ಭೋಜನವನಿಂತು ಮಾಡುತ್ತಿರ್ದರಾ ಪಾರ್ವರು ||
ಓಗರವ ತಾ ತೊಗೆಯನಿಕ್ಕು ಹಸನಾಯ್ತು ಮೇ|
ಲೋಗರವ ಬಡಿಸು ದೊನ್ನೆಗಳು ಹಿಡಿವಂತೆ ಯುಂ|
ಟಾಗಿ ಹೆರೆದುಪ್ಪವೆಱೆಯಾಸಳಿದ್ಬಮನಿಟ್ಟು ಕಲಸುವೋಗರವ ತೋಟಾ ||
ಬೇಗದಿಂದೆಡೆಮಾಡಿದಿಡ್ಡಲಿಗೆ ದೋಸೆಗಳ|
ಮೇಗೆ ಸಕ್ಕರೆ ಬಟ್ಟವಾಲ ಹೊಯ್ಯೆನುತಮಾ|
ರೋಗಣೆಯನಾ ಪೊಟ್ಟೆಯೊಡೆವ ಮರ್ಯಾದೆಯೊಳಗುಂಡು ತೇಗುತ್ತಿರ್ದರು ||

ಪಾಯಸದ ಪರಿಗಳಂ ನೋಡಿ ಪಂಡಿತರೆ ನವ|
ಯಾಯಿತೇ ಉಯ್ಯುಪಾಧ್ಯಾಯರೇ ಕರಜಿಗೆಯ |
ಕಾಯ ದೋಸೆಗಳ ಹಸನಂ ಪುರೋಹಿತರೇ ಚೆನ್ನಾಗಿ ಸವಿಸವಿದು ನೋಡಿ ||
ಈ ಯೆಗ್ಗೊಯೂರಿಗೆಯ ಮೃದುತರಕೆ ಸರಿಯುಂಟೆ |
ಜೋಯಿಸರೆ ಕೇಳಿ ಸಕ್ಕರೆಯುರುಡೆಗಳ ನಸ್ಮ |
ಬಾಯ ಬಿಡಿಸಂ ಬಿಡಿಸುತಿಹ ದೀಕ್ಷಿತರೆ ಬಂದು ಕೊಂಡಾಡುತಿರ್ದಾಗ ||

(II. 188)

In conclusion I have to offer my cordial thanks to the Mysore University for giving me an opportunity to deliver these lectures.

INDEX[1]

[1] Compiled by Mr. M. Hanumantha Rao, B.A. (Hons.)

[1] Italicised figures are inscription numbers; roman figures are page references.